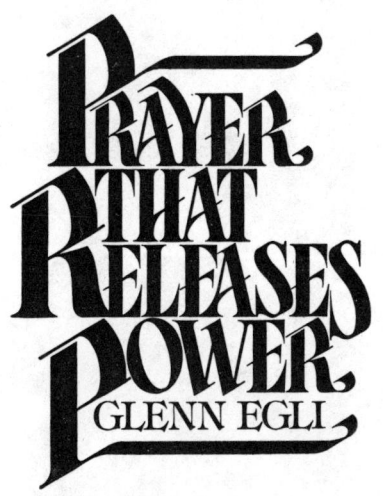

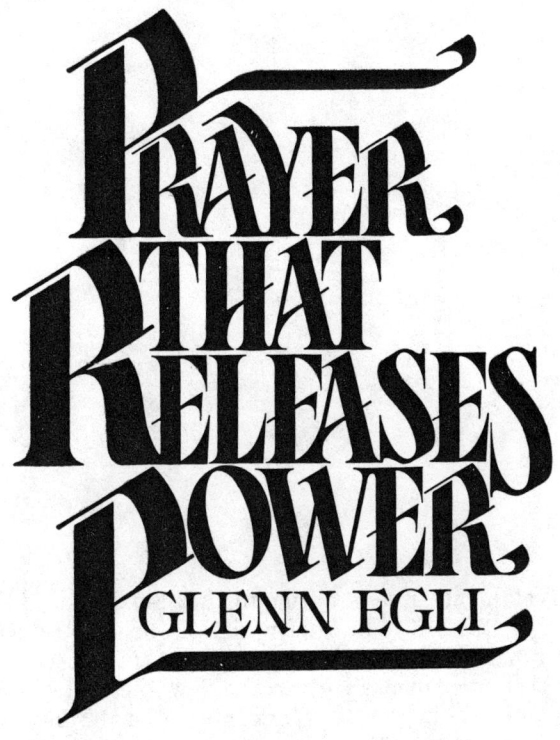

Bridge Publishing, Inc.
Plainfield, N.J.

Old Testament quotes are from the Revised Standard Version, copyright © 1952, 1971 by the Division of Christian Education of the Churches of Christ in the United States of America.
New Testament quotes are from the New International Version, copyright © 1978 by the New York International Bible Society.
Italicized portions of Scripture are the author's italics.

PRAYER THAT RELEASES POWER
Copyright © 1982 by Bridge Publishing, Inc.
Printed in the United States of America
Library of Congress Catalog Number: 81-71753
International Standard Book Number: 0-88270-506-7
Bridge Publishing, Inc., Plainfield, New Jersey 07060

Acknowledgments

I want to thank the following for their help in making this book possible: Kenton Showalter, for his affirmation of the concept and for his personal encouragement; Joanne Nice, for her patience in typing and retyping the manuscript; Souderton Mennonite Church, for making Joanne's services available; and Art McPhee for his friendship and editorial help.

Preface

Jesus says: "I tell you the truth, if you have faith and do not doubt, . . . you can say to this mountain, 'Go, throw yourself into the sea,' and it will be done. If you believe, you will receive whatever you ask for in prayer" (Matt. 21:21, 22). *Prayer That Releases Power*, by my friend and former co-worker, Glenn Egli, is an exciting book that calls us back to the words of Jesus. It reminds us to relearn what it means to approach the throne of grace boldly.

However, more than that, this useful and authoritative manual is a practical guidebook to expectant praying that will revolutionize the prayer lives of many. Glenn Egli has been teaching these concepts for years now, and his teaching has already had amazing results. Homes have been saved, scars from the past have been healed, negative attitudes and emotions have been overcome, and physical healings have been common. That is why many of Glenn's seminar participants, parishioners, and friends have been urging him to publish this already-tested manuscript for wider distribution. Glenn's call to bold profession of the promises of God is much needed, and I know of nothing else quite like this helpful volume for motivating lethargic

Christians to action.

Any Christian who takes seriously the fact that Jesus came to give us access to God knows that nothing is more important in the Christian life than prayer. With R.A. Torrey, he or she is driven to say, "I must pray, pray, pray. I must put all my energy and heart into prayer. Whatever else I do, I must pray." *Prayer That Releases Power* helps us do that in four ways: first, it helps us see the need for bold profession; secondly, it challenges us to exercise the faith God has given us; thirdly, it shows us the potential by highlighting many of the astounding promises of God's Word in a helpful topical arrangement; and fourthly, it helps us to act by giving us actual illustrations (or models) of prayers of profession.

I have often dreamed of the amazing potential of a Church which has recovered its lost sense of the power of prayer. We Christians simply cannot fathom the potential impact of the unreleased power of God that's at our disposal. There is power for changing lives, for revitalizing the churches, for transforming the world! More than ever before, we need to recapture a high view of prayer. But even more than that, we need to put that vision into action. We need to put into motion the prayer of faith that moves the arm of God. I believe this manual will encourage many to do just that.

Arthur G. McPhee,
May, 1980

Arthur G. McPhee is the author of *Friendship Evangelism, Traveling Light,* and *Making Friends For God.*

Contents

Introduction	1
Exercised Faith	9
Prayers of Petition	11
1. Confession and Profession	12
2. Praying in a Dead Sphere	14
3. Praying the Problems Instead of the Answers	15
God's Word Is God's Will	17
Ingredients of Prayers of Petition	21
1. Extracting Facts	21
2. Exercising Faith	21
3. Exorcising Feelings	24
Praying Prayers of Petition	25
Index	115

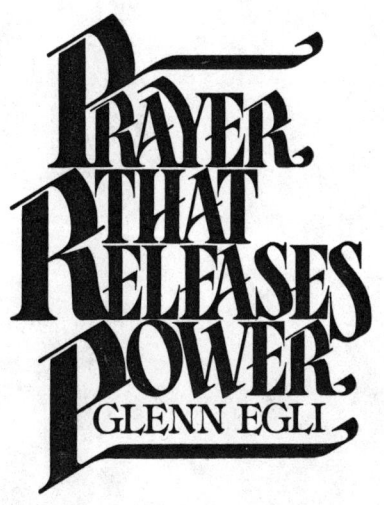

Introduction

"What are you so excited about?" asked my friend.
"You can tell?" I said.
"Tell?" he replied. "You've done everything but leap into the air! You've been beaming ever since you got here this afternoon. And it's been obvious you're bursting for an opportunity to tell me about something."
"Maybe I've been soaking in too much of that long overdue sunshine," I teased.
Both of us gazed across the meadow at the late afternoon sun getting ready to settle down upon the blue hills of the Shenandoah Valley. The sun wove beautiful shades of green along the sides of the mountain wherever its light penetrated the clouds. The cumulus clouds themselves were big puffy billows, and the sky formed a backdrop of pure blue. It was indeed an exciting kind of afternoon in and of itself, one of God's more extravagant displays—but that wasn't it. That wasn't what I was beaming about, and we both knew it.
"It's about Abe," I said. "I was in to see him last night. He had three heart attacks while you were away, and he seemed to be taking another turn for the worst."

"I heard."

"Well, last night Abe asked some of us to come and anoint him with oil and pray with him. And while we were praying, all at once the promise from Ezekiel 36:26 came into my mind. You know the one I mean: 'A new heart will I give you. . . .' And God seemed to be saying to me, 'Claim the promise.' "

"Did you do it?"

"Well, at first I resisted, because that promise refers to spiritual renewal in its context. But God seemed to be saying I should claim it for Abe for physical healing, so I did—and that's what I'm so excited about! Mabel, Abe's wife, called this morning to say the doctor had just been in to see Abe and was astounded by the change. He left the room saying he wouldn't be surprised to see Abe return to block-laying within a few months. Isn't that great? That's what I call a real miracle!"

I expected my friend to be as excited by the news as I was, but he was strangely silent. He gazed off across the meadow again and said, without looking at me, "When I pray, nothing ever happens!"

Abe did return to block-laying, and since that day I have seen God come through again and again when I've claimed the promises in His Word. But since that day, I've also met dozens of persons like my friend, whose petitions have not met with positive results. I think I know why.

I've quizzed my friends about their petitions, and I've discovered a revealing difference between those whose prayers are answered and those whose prayers are not. Put simply, the bottom line is this: Few Christians have learned how to pray in a truly biblical way, to effectively wield "the sword of the Spirit, which is the word of God" (Eph. 6:17).

I used to be in that position. I saw prayer working, but I didn't know how. When I was eighteen, I was stricken with polio. Inch by inch my paralysis spread, and my lungs began to be affected. The doctors wanted to put me in an iron lung, but my parents wanted an opportunity to call our local church to prayer in my behalf first. They put out the word immediately, and I know there were dozens of people praying that night. And God heard their requests. The next morning there was a marked improvement. And, before long, there was complete recovery. However, even though I knew there was a distinct connection between the prayers of those people and my return to a healthy state, I did not know how to pray for positive results.

I had a first cousin who did though. His name was Roy, and I was impressed even then by his dynamic Christian faith. Sometimes his testimonies about the miraculous and powerful ways God was working seemed far-out to me. I thought he was a bit extreme. But there was a genuineness and sincerity about him that had me convinced there was *something* more to prayer than I was experiencing, although I could not put my finger on what that "something" was just then.

A lot of my confusion boiled down to the difference between faith and works. When I prayed, I was relying on my act of praying, rather than on the faithfulness of God. I didn't realize it then, but it was *my* activity that seemed important; God's was secondary. Merely praying was what was important, when, instead, I should have been exercising faith that God would be true to His promises. I would never have admitted it, but my manner of praying was ignoring Jesus' plain statement: "Apart from *me* you can do nothing."

Christians live dynamic lives to the degree that God's Word is released through their lives. "In the beginning was the Word, and the Word was with God, and the Word was God" (John 1:1). That Scripture describes Jesus, the living Word. But God's written Word is a living Word too. It is far more than mere words. God says the Lord Jesus is "sustaining all things by his powerful word" (Heb. 1:3). He says His Word is alive and powerful. The day I discovered that is the day I discovered how to refocus my prayers, to begin exercising faith by laying hold of God's power through professing His promises.

This way of releasing the power behind the promises came home to me when I was reading 2 Peter 1:3, 4:

> His divine power has given us everything we need for life and godliness through our knowledge of him who called us by his own glory and goodness. Through these he has given us his very great and precious promises, so that through them you may participate in the divine nature and escape the corruption in the world. . . .

What a marvelous discovery that was to me. I could participate in God's very nature—see it released into my own life—by simply acting on His promises, by trusting their veracity and by claiming (professing) them.

Let me show you how this works in my prayer life. Suppose I read in God's Word: "In him we have redemption through his blood, the forgiveness of sins. . . ." (Eph. 1:7). As I consider this promise from God, the truth breaks through to my spirit that Jesus, through His shed blood, has redeemed me out of the hands of the devil and I am forgiven! Therefore, I can profess in prayer, "Heavenly Father, according to Ephesians 1:7, through the blood of Jesus I am redeemed out of the hands of the devil, and that's not all—I am forgiven of all my sins!" And as I make that profession in prayer, the power of that promise is released into my life and becomes a personal reality.

While I was in college, I made a second important discovery about God's Word for my life. First Corinthians 15:42-45 expresses the essence of it:

> The body that is sown is perishable, it is raised imperishable; it is sown in dishonor, it is raised in glory; it is sown in weakness, it is raised in power; it is sown a natural body, it is raised a spiritual body.
>
> If there is a natural body, there is also a spiritual body. So it is written: "The first man Adam became a living being,"; the last Adam [Christ], a life-giving spirit.

In other words, every believer has a spiritual nature, which has been brought to life by the Holy Spirit. The nonbeliever knows nothing of this. He only knows there is an emptiness within, a void, a "God-shaped vacuum," as Augustine put it. But the believer has literally become a new person. He is no longer merely a physical being but a spiritual one as well. "Therefore, if anyone is in Christ, he is a new creation; the old has gone, the new has come!" (2 Cor. 5:17).

Now, just as our physical bodies fade and die if they are not fed, even so our spiritual bodies wither away when they are not fed. And a lot of Christians are starving spiritually because they do not feed their spiritual bodies.

Satan tempted the Lord Jesus by saying, "If you are the Son of God, tell these stones to become bread." After a fast of forty days, that must have seemed an enticing course. But Jesus was the Son of God, so He replied, "It is written: 'Man does not live on bread alone, but on every word that comes from the mouth of God'" (Matt. 4:3, 4). In doing this Jesus taught us two things: First, He taught us the principle of releasing divine power (through professing the Word of God) to defeat Satan; secondly, He taught us the principle of spiritual sustenance by feeding on and filling ourselves with the Father's Word. Another time Jesus said, "My flesh is real food and my blood is real drink" (John 6:55). Commenting on this saying, He added: "The words I have spoken to you are spirit and they are life" (John 6:63b). Christ, the Word made flesh, is saying the Word is real food. And followers of Christ need to learn how to feed on, not just read, the Word of God. For only when we're full of the Word do we have the spiritual discernment and vitality to employ the Word as Jesus did.

Jesus knew Satan stood no chance when He released the divine energy of God. Rational thinking would not have understood that. But Jesus, and any Christian who is full of the Word of God, does not face a circumstance like that with a purely intellectual frame of mind. He moves beyond rational thinking to spiritual thinking.

For example, when I face an ill person in a hospital room, I look around at the attending doctors and nurses and say, "What am I doing here?" My intellect says, "What good will it do for me to pray? I'll only make a fool of myself. What if God doesn't answer?" But then I move beyond rational thinking to spiritual thinking, and I say to my intellect, "It is written in Isaiah 53:5:

> But he was wounded for our transgressions, he was bruised for our iniquities; upon him was the chastisement that made us whole, and with his stripes we are healed."

I can then move with all assurance to the bedside of the suffering person and pray, "In the name of Jesus, according to Isaiah 53:5, I say to you, be healed." And God will heal the person in that bed in His own time and way: one time physically, one time spiritually (the greatest healing), perhaps another time mentally. Sometimes God heals immediately; other times He kills the disease and allows the body to heal by natural processes. But He does heal! My intellect tells me it's nonsense, but my spirit trusts the truthfulness of God's Word unquestioningly. Upon the basis of the promise in God's Word, I make a profession, and God's power to heal is released.

Now, I can't emphasize enough the importance of moving beyond rational thinking to spiritual thinking in this whole matter. Spiritual thinking is not irrational thinking, however. Spiritual thinking is merely the acceptance of the fact that God's ways are not our ways and that God's thoughts are not our thoughts. He thinks and acts on a far higher level than we do. He is not limited as we are. Therefore, we move beyond logical expectations and take God at His Word.

Far too often we don't do that though. The reading of God's Word becomes merely the feeding of our intellects. We fill our minds with its content only, and let it lie there like grass in the cud of a cow. Instead, we need to digest the Word of God. But digestion of the Word of God takes place only in the spirit.

Hebrews 4:12 highlights the division between human thinking and spiritual thinking. It shows how the Word of God, when properly received, divides between the two: "The word of God is living and active. Sharper than any double-edged sword, it penetrates even to dividing soul and spirit. . . ." "Living and *active*. . . ." The Greek word for "active" is *energy*. God is saying, "My Word is active and energizing! It penetrates even to the dividing of soul and spirit." The Greek word for "soul" is *psyche*, the human capacity for reasoning (rational thinking). So, the Word of God separates rational thinking from spiritual thinking.

But why does the Word separate the two? Why is that important? Simply because Christians need to make their decisions on the basis of spiritual thinking. Often, our Bibles translate a person's "spirit" as "heart." But, of course, that doesn't mean our spirit is the same thing as the pumping mechanism in our chest. When I tell my wife, "I love you with all my heart," I'm not saying, "I love you with all my pumping muscle." No, no! I'm talking about that part of my being that ultimately makes all my decisions.

Let me put it this way: My human intellect is not really the decision-maker of my being. I may sometimes think of it that way, but it is not really. My intellect stores, sorts, and analyzes data, but my spirit compares the data with the Word of God and makes the decisions that are translated into action.

That is why the Bible teaches: "Trust in the Lord with all your heart [spirit], and do not rely on your own insight [intellect]" (Prov. 3:5). We need to move beyond rational thinking to spiritual thinking. We need to compare the Word with regard to present circumstances and past experiences. We need to act on the basis of the Word and not merely on what seems logical. We need to exercise faith in the power of the Word, regarding it "not as the word of men, but as it actually is, the word of God. . ." (1 Thess. 2:13).

Look at this amplified statement of 1 Thessalonians 2:13, as an even clearer highlighting of what I mean:

> And we also thank God continually because you received the Word of God's message not as the word of men, but for what it really is, the Word of God which becomes energized in you as you exercise faith.

Notice, God's Word comes alive (is energized in us) as we exercise faith in its truthfulness and power. It is not understood intellectually but "stood under"—"received." But what does it mean to "exercise faith?"

Exercised Faith

Faith is a gift. "For it is by grace you have been saved, through faith—and this not from yourselves, it is the gift of God. . ." (Eph. 2:8). God gives us faith so we can obtain mercy (grace).

Who receives this gift of faith? Romans 12:3 makes it clear: "For by the grace given me I say to *every one of you:* Do not think of yourself more highly than you ought, but. . . with the measure of faith God has given you." The King James Version puts it like this: ". . . as God hath dealt *to every man* the measure of faith." The answer to the question, "To whom is faith given?" is this: *everyone!* Faith is a gift of God given to every person.

This raises a second question: How much faith is given to every person? The same amount? Varying amounts? I remember a woman who used to respond to invitations to receive healing at meeting after meeting. She desperately wanted to receive healing, but she never seemed to get it. One evening she said to the minister in charge of anointing, "Please pray for me before you anoint me, and ask God to give me more faith. I've come forward for healing many times, but I just don't seem to have enough faith."

The woman was startled by the word of wisdom God then gave the minister. "Sister," he said, "your problem is not that you don't have enough faith. Your problem is that you don't use the faith you have."

The minister was right. How much faith does God give? "And God is faithful; he will not let you be tempted beyond what you can bear. But when you are tempted, he will also provide a way out so that you can stand up under it" (1 Cor. 10:13). The answer is, God gives each person *enough* faith!

When I was nineteen, I moved to Chicago. I had found a job there, and I moved in with a group of young men who gambled heavily on the football games. One day they asked me to drive them to a certain location to place their bets. I knew it was wrong, but I half-heartedly agreed. I did not want to give my new friends the impression I was a "goody-goody." And besides, I loved gambling too.

I was supposed to drive them to the location the next day. That night I prayed, "Heavenly Father, I have two weaknesses to contend with tomorrow: I enjoy gambling and I want to impress my new friends." Then I claimed 1 Corinthians 10:13, that God would not give me a test too big for me. The next day the fellows I was rooming with came to me and said they'd found another car. God was true to His word, and I had taken one small step in learning to exercise faith in it.

Put simply, to exercise faith means to decide in my spirit to act according to God's Word, even when logic seems to suggest a different course of action. My intellect told me I didn't have the inner strength to resist gambling with my roommates. So, I set faith in motion by deciding 1 Corinthians 10:13 was true for me and by professing it to be so.

You may be thinking that the sudden availability of another car was an easy way out of my gambling dilemma, that it would have been better if God had given me the inner strength to deal with it. I grant you that, but let me add this: once I began to exercise faith in the manner I've recounted, little by little God gave me the inner resolve to deal with many weaknesses. By learning to exercise faith through professing God's Word to be true for me, I had launched out into a new journey of the human spirit. With the Bible as my prayer book, I had discovered a new power base, a new source of energy. And little by little I found my values changing, my desires changing—more and more, I found my will coming into harmony with God's will.

There's a line in the musical *The Sound of Music*, which goes: "I have confidence in confidence alone." That may be a good lyric but it's horrible theology. Many Christians have faith in faith, but until they learn to exercise faith, God's will and their will are not going to line up. The power to love a holy life and to display the fruit of the Spirit (God's own characteristics) in their living, will be an impossibility. It will also be impossible for them to immerse themselves in the work God wants them to do, because spiritual work demands spiritual power.

It is interesting to observe that in the New Testament, "faith" is often a participle or verb instead of a noun. Much of the time it would be more properly translated "faithing" or "exercised faith." Faith is not faith unless it is faith in action. Faith is not a noun but a verb.

Prayers of Petition

That brings me to the purpose of this book. I believe that by professing the promises of God in His Word, we can receive power: power for overcoming the forces of evil that work contrary to the will of God; power for overcoming our own sinful tendencies. By exercising faith in this way, we can release God's living, powerful

Word and experience ongoing transformation, so that more and more we become conformed to the image of Christ. Therefore, my purpose is to show you how these concepts can revolutionize your prayer life, specifically your prayers of petition.

First, though, let's look at some roadblocks to answered prayer.

1. *Confession and Profession*

In the New Testament, confession and profession are the same word: *homologeo*. This word is a combination of two Greek words: *homo*, meaning "the same as"; and *logeo*, meaning "the Word." Confession and profession mean to say words that are the same as (or are in agreement with) God's Word. The distinction in English is according to context. Confession is negative, having to do with sin. Profession is positive, acknowledging the truthfulness of God's Word concerning His provision. But in the Greek they are the same word, which suggests two things: first, confession and profession ought almost to be thought of in the same breath—they go together; secondly, confession ought, probably, to be seen in a more positive way than we usually view it.

First of all, whenever we profess the promises of God, we confess our own limitations and sinfulness. To do otherwise is impossible. To lay hold of God's power through positive profession is to acknowledge our own inability due to sin. However, the trouble is that while such acknowledgment is implicit, seldom do we make it a conscious acknowledgment. We need to do that though—to approach Him always with a profound sense of our smallness and sinfulness, and, on the other hand, with a deep awareness of His greatness and graciousness.

But such confession is positive. It is positive because,

combined with professing the promises of the Word, it brings healing and wholeness. And it is positive, because it brings glory to Jesus, who died so that we *could* confess our sins and be forgiven.

In *The Broken Wall*, Markus Barth reminds us that the rabbis spoke of confession in precisely that way, as giving God the glory. (Notice, for example, John 9:24.) In true confession the glory of Jesus is revealed. When Isaiah said, "Woe is me! . . . my eyes have seen the King," the focus was not only on his sin, but God's glory. When Peter said, "Go away from me, Lord; I am a sinful man!", the focus was not only on his sinfulness, but Jesus' glory. That is always the way of it with true confession. It is inspired by His glory, and it highlights His glory.

A few years ago, my brother Joe told me how he prays. He said each time he prays, he retreats in his mind to a favorite room. It is a small room with no windows or doors, but it is comfortably decorated with his favorite things. In his mind, he goes to the room and finds Jesus waiting there. Then, he and Jesus sit down and talk together, just the two of them.

I decided to try the same thing. I prayed in that manner for several weeks, when, one day, Jesus appeared to me in a new way. In my mind, I had entered into my favorite room to fellowship with Jesus, just as usual. But this time He shown with an awesome radiance and glory! It was utterly dazzling and overwhelming. My whole being was overcome with His glory. I felt just like Isaiah must have felt. I remember falling to the floor, and I remember how black my sins seemed in the light of His glory. I was too ashamed to even look upon Him. But Jesus came to me, placed His hand upon me, and said, "Glenn, it's all right. My blood has made you clean. I love you." Then, Jesus took my hands, lifted me up, wrapped His arms around me, and hugged me. "You are free," he said. "Free to worship the Father. Free to praise."

There was confession in that moment, but the confession was also praise—a free acknowledging of the greatness and grandeur and glory of Jesus. And the power of God flowed through me, bringing tears which seemed like a cleansing river flowing through and over me.

2. *Praying in a Dead Sphere*

So, there must be conscious confession as well as profession. There must also be an immersing of one's self into the rarefied atmosphere of the Holy Spirit.

Here is what I mean. In 1 Corinthians 2:16, Paul says we have "the mind of Christ." A few years ago, I was reflecting on those words and decided to check out the meaning of "mind." I discovered its meaning in Paul's day was completely different than its meaning today. Today's equivalent would be more like "sphere" or "realm." So, what Paul was actually saying was this: When we become Christians, we occupy a different realm—a spiritual one.

Awhile back, I took a friend, Al, for an airplane ride. I had just received my pilot's license, and I was eager to take him up. Al wasn't so eager though, so I was ever so careful to lift the aircraft very smoothly into the air. I used a slow rate of climb so as not to frighten Al, but suddenly he grabbed my arm and said, "Look, look!" I didn't know what had happened. I thought maybe the engine was on fire or that maybe we'd lost a wheel. But to my delight, I discovered Al was simply expressing his amazement at the sight of an Illinois cornfield from the air. It was a totally new perspective for him, and he was thrilled.

Just so, when Paul speaks of having the mind of Christ, he is referring to the fact that we now have a new perspective. Our horizons have been expanded. We are enabled to see our lives and this world a little more as God sees them. We have something of what Peter Marshall used to call "the long view." In Romans 12, the Apostle Paul refers to it as the renewing of our minds.

But, even though as Christians our minds have been renewed, it is possible to go back to the old way of seeing and to pray from that limited perspective. Whenever we do that, our petitions will not achieve positive results. Sometimes, we try to live in both realms, and there, too, our petitions will go unanswered. James calls it double-mindedness. He says, "That man should not think he will receive anything from the Lord" (1:7).

3. *Praying the Problems Instead of the Answers*

Here is still another roadblock to effective prayer. It describes a kind of praying that might better be classified as mourning. Many Christians approach God as though the crucifixion and resurrection had never happened. They come to God in a lugubrious mood, when they should be coming to Him in a celebrative mood. Instead of expecting to lay hold of the power of the risen Christ within them, they come complaining and expecting defeat. They expect it, and they get it.

That is not what God wants at all, of course. In fact, it is a great insult to the God who stepped into human history in the person of Jesus Christ, and who was crucified, for us to pray like that. It is a denial of the effectiveness of His sacrifice to give us access once again to His throne room. One can only conclude, upon hearing such Christians pray, that they are altogether ignorant of their privilege of entering the presence of God through the shed blood of Christ.

But, according to Hebrews 10:19-23, it shouldn't be that way, but just the reverse:

> Therefore, brothers, since we have confidence to enter the Most Holy Place by the blood of Jesus, by a new and living way opened for us through the curtain, that is, his body, and since we have a great priest over the house of God, let us draw near to God with a sincere heart in full assurance of faith, having our hearts sprinkled to cleanse us from a guilty conscience and having our bodies washed with pure water. Let us hold unswervingly to the hope we *profess*, for he who promised is faithful.

When we come into God's presence, we needn't come in doubt or defeat. We can come boldly, focusing on answers, not problems. In fact, we can profess answers to all our problems, for the answers to all the problems we face are to be found in God's Word. For example, while the Word of God will not tell me which specific job to take, it does address itself to the heart of my concern: "Trust in the Lord with all your heart [spirit], and do not rely on your own insight [intellect]; In all your ways acknowledge him, and he will make straight your paths" (Prov. 3:5, 6).

Many persons fail in prayer because they do not know what God's Word says. Therefore, they focus their petition on their problem because they have no promise to base it upon. God's Word is God's will. If we know what His Word promises, we know His will.

When I was a young Christian, I was frequently guilty of the very thing I've been talking about. I remember often praying problem-centered prayers like this: "Heavenly Father, I feel lousy this morning, and it looks like another one of those miserable, hot days again. Father, you know I've been having trouble with my employees and that I'm fed up to my neck with George. And, Lord, on top of it all, the kids seem to be coming down with something. Oh! And the car acts like it may break down. And, oh yes, I'm not enjoying those special meetings at church one bit. I must go now, Lord. Help me today. In Jesus' name, amen."

Today, however, my prayers are different. Today, I profess divine health according to Matthew 8:17. I profess the blood of Jesus over my children to protect them from illness. I profess that according to 1 Corinthians 10:13, no trial will come upon me today that is greater than I can handle. And I profess that according to Romans 8:15, God has put His Holy Spirit within me, and because He longs and loves to praise the Father, I will enjoy every worship service.

In the old days, I imagine the Lord heard my complaining prayers and said, "Be it unto Glenn according to his words." Now, I believe the Father smiles and says, "Be it unto Glenn according to *my* Word!"

God's Word Is God's Will

In his book, *Releasing the Ability of God*, Charles Capp writes, "Prayer is to line ourselves up with the Word of God and set ourselves in a position to give God liberty to move on our behalf." To that I would add only this: We must not only line ourselves up with God's Word, but act on it by claiming its promises. When we make a profession in prayer (one based on the Word of God), we are speaking faith-filled words. We are exercising faith. And God says His Word will never return to Him without its divine energy potential being released:

> For as the rain and snow come down from heaven, and return not thither but water the earth, making it bring forth and sprout, giving seed to the sower and bread to the eater, so shall my word be that goes forth from my mouth; it shall not return to me empty, but it shall accomplish what which I purpose, and prosper in the thing for which I sent it. (Isa. 55:10, 11)

Now, it is important that we realize that God's way is not always our way. Nor is His timetable always our timetable. We must constantly bear in mind that God's delay is not God's denial. However, when we profess the Word of God in a right attitude, we know God hears our prayers, even though we may not always see the results immediately. As John says:

> This is the assurance we have in approaching God: that if we ask anything according to his will [and, remember, His Word is His will], he hears us. And if we know that he hears us—whatever we ask—we know that we have what we asked of him. (1 John 5:14, 15)

By "faithing" we know that we already have the answer to what we asked, because we have prayed in accordance with the Word of God. We might not see the answer for a season; nevertheless, we know it is forthcoming.

For example, when I pray for healing based on verses like Matthew 8:17, 1 Peter 2:24, or Isaiah 53:5, God heals. The question is not *whether* He will heal, but *how* He will heal. He may heal the person physically—instantly. He may heal the person spiritually. He may heal through normal bodily processes. He may heal through the channel of trained medical personnel. He may even heal perfectly, permanently—through death.

To assume God must always heal in one of those ways and not the others is presumption, not faith. It is His option, not ours. But the praying one asks expectantly, knowing that on the basis of God's Word, the appropriate form of healing will come.

By the power of the Word, we know we can face every trial we encounter: "And God is faithful; he will not let you be tempted beyond what you can bear. But when you are tempted, he will also provide a way out so that you can stand up under it (1 Cor. 10:13). What is the way out? Normally, it is God's own Word. We may be tested beyond our own strength to endure, but we will never be tested beyond the resources God has provided.

For years I struggled with being overweight. I carried around about twenty extra pounds. I really believe Satan was testing me. I tried several methods of losing weight. All proved temporary at best. But one day I remembered that the last fruit of the Holy Spirit listed in Galatians 5:23 is self under control. So, I confessed to God that the temptation to eat wrong foods was more than I could handle. However, I did not stop there. I went on to profess that the Holy Spirit was living in me and that one of His fruits for my life was self-control. I told the Father I was going to claim that power of self-control, and God honored that profession and continues to every day I allow Him.

I have always liked the way this secret to unlocking divine resources is described in John 15. The Lord is the speaker:

> If you remain in me and my words remain in you, ask whatever you wish, and it will be given you. This is to my Father's glory, that you bear much fruit, showing yourselves to be my disciples. (vv. 7, 8)

That is, when God's Word is received as truth by us, and lives in us, then we ask and receive according to it. And the result? We bear fruit, and God is glorified. As we bear fruit, we show ourselves to be His disciples.

The Psalmist knew the value of God's living Word within. He wrote, "I have laid up thy word in my heart [spirit], that I might not sin against thee" (Ps. 119:11). How did he do it? By listening to portions of God's Word until the truth became real, by allowing God to animate the promises of the Word in his spirit.

We are to do the same: meditating on the verse or passage, we allow it to sink in deeply; then, we profess its truthfulness to the Father, relying on the Holy Spirit to help us recall it when it coincides with our need.

If, in that way, we do not allow God's Word to become a part of us, alive in us, we have only the flesh—our intellects—to draw upon. And there is no guarantee whatever that a decision is a right one merely because it is a rational one. Furthermore, even if it is a right decision, it is not a faith decision, and, therefore, we will be left to our own feeble resources to carry it out. I made the decision to lose weight many times, but until I made the decision on the basis of God's living Word within, I did not have the power to carry it out. I was making a rational decision, which was okay as far as it went; but I needed to move beyond rational thinking to spiritual thinking to experience God's help.

What is true of relying on intellect alone is also true of relying on feelings alone. Our feelings may prove right, but they do not, by themselves, determine truth; God's Word is truth. "God is spirit, and his worshipers must worship *in spirit* and in truth" (John 4:24). Reliance on rational thinking or feelings does not release divine energy in our lives; only exercising faith in God's Word does.

Ingredients of Prayers of Petition

Answered prayer depends on three decisions: (1) a decision to believe God's Word; (2) a decision to profess it as true and relevant to the need, plus a willingness to act on it; (3) a decision to override intellect and especially feelings when they are not in harmony with what Scripture indicates our response should be. Let's look at them one at a time:

1. *Extracting Facts*
The first decision for answered prayer is the determination to separate fact from fiction. We must resolve to find out what the Word says about every need we take to the Lord. We must decide to trust God's Word as the one sure foundation upon which to build, to determine to extract its wisdom—the only really vital facts—about every petitionary matter. With the inspired writers of old, we must agree: "For ever, O Lord, thy word is firmly fixed in the heavens" (Ps. 119:89); "The grass withers, the flower fades; but the word of our God will stand for ever" (Isa. 40:8). And we must come to embrace Jesus' statement: "If you hold to my teaching [His Word], you are really my disciples. Then you will know the truth, and the truth will set you free" (John 8:31, 32).

2. *Exercising Faith*
But beyond getting the facts to base our petitions on, we need to employ what the Bible says regarding the request we are making. It is one thing to find the promises in the Word; it is another thing to claim them. It is one thing to hear what Scripture has to say about a matter; but, as Jesus said, it is another thing to heed it. The facts must be recognized; then, faith must

be exercised!

Before studying for the ministry I was a carpenter for twelve years in Illinois. The last six years I was also involved in screen process printing. When I left the business world and began my ministerial studies, I discovered a weakness that had never come to light before. I became discouraged because our financial self-reliance had been undercut. Along with the strain of a heavy school load came the strain of financial uncertainty, and depression began to overwhelm me. I claimed God would meet all my needs in Christ Jesus (Phil. 4:19), but apparently God wanted me to see something more, because I still could not shake the frustration I felt. I began to feel ashamed that I, a minister, should find myself in such a state. I began to feel guilty as well as frustrated. But then I came across these verses:

> Therefore, since we have a great high priest who has gone through the heavens, Jesus the Son of God, let us hold firmly to the faith we profess. For we do not have a high priest who is unable to sympathize with our weaknesses, but we have one who has been tempted in every way, just as we are—yet was without sin. Let us then approach the throne of grace with confidence, so that we may receive mercy and find grace to help us in our time of need. (Heb. 4:14-16)

I listened as God spoke to me through these words from Hebrews, and I realized what mattered was not the sinfulness of my worry but the fact that Jesus understood! It was up to me to approach the throne of grace with confidence and there receive mercy and find grace. As this truth became real to me, I went to God on the basis of it, asking God to forgive me and give me strength. I came away with new freedom. I felt clean, at peace, full of joy. God had stood by His promise once more. He *had* understood my weakness, and He had bathed me in His mercy and grace. I could not help coming away from the experience praising His name!

I want to highlight a very important principle involved in the story I've just recounted. It is a vital principle for all petitionary prayer. When we exercise faith in the promises of God, it is imperative that we profess our confidence in the Word *verbally*. That is an essential part of setting faith in motion. Romans 10:8-10 makes it plain. It tells us that we must not only internalize the Word, but we must verbalize it too: "'The word is near you; it is in your mouth and in your heart,' that is, the word of faith we are proclaiming: That if you confess *with your mouth*. . . ."

The idea, of course, is not that there is something magical about articulating the promises. Rather, it is this: what has come home to us through the Word must be acted upon. It is not enough to realize the facts; we must step out in faith (through a concrete act) for those facts to become reality in our experience. That is the difference between real faith and mere intellectual assent. If someone offers me a dollar, the dollar is potentially mine but not actually mine until I reach out and receive it. In the same way, the promises are potentially mine—and I may fully realize that—but not actually mine until a concrete step of faith (profession) has been taken.

But even that is not enough. Exercising faith requires obedience as well as profession. James says, ". . . faith by itself, if it is not accompanied by action, is dead" (2:17). Romans 1:5 makes it clear that that "action" also includes obedience: "Through him and for his name's sake, we received grace and apostleship to call people from among the Gentiles to *the obedience that comes from faith.*"

The word obedience has roots that refer to opening a door or responding to a knock (see Acts 12:13). We may profess and profess and never receive, because God expects the action of profession to be backed up by the action of obedience. So, opening the door that allows the energy of God to flow into our lives is the result of a decision to act on two levels: profession and obedience. As James says of Abraham: "You see that his faith and his actions were working together, and his faith was complete by what he did" (2:22).

3. *Exorcising Feelings*

Often Satan keeps us from acting on the promises of God's Word by planting seeds of doubt in us. If we are prone at all to depend upon our intellects or feelings in finally making a decision, he is ready for us. I think pointing out the latter is especially important. I have been amazed at how many people—Christian people!—make major decisions on the basis of their feelings. For example, there is a man in our town who is probably the epitome of a negative thinker. Suggest anything new, propose any change, make any challenge, set any goal, and he will find half a dozen potential reasons why it won't work. And he is quite unwilling to move ahead because of his negative vibes. But feelings aren't supposed to control us; we are supposed to control our feelings, in this sense at least: we can reject negative feelings when they aren't in harmony with the Word of God by refusing to receive them. We need only recognize that those negative feelings are not God's will for us to have. God wants us to act on the basis of facts (His Word), not feelings (due to circumstances). Feelings constantly change; God's Word never changes.

Take the matter of forgiveness. In my ministry I often run across folks who are shackled by bitterness and unforgiveness. And the two always go together. Because of bitterness (feelings), they refuse to forgive. But I have not found one verse of Scripture that says we must feel like forgiving. There are many verses of Scripture, however, that command us to forgive. And John 20:21-23 makes it clear God gives the Holy Spirit to enable us to forgive. In the Parable of the Unmerciful Servant, Jesus says that the servant's master turned him over to the jailors until he repaid all he owed. He adds: "This is how my heavenly Father will treat each of you unless you forgive your brother from your heart" (Matt. 18:35). In another place Jesus says: "For if you forgive men when they sin against you, your heavenly Father will also forgive you. But if you do not forgive men their sins, your Father will not forgive your sins" (Matt. 6:14, 15). So, when someone says to me, "I just don't feel like forgiving; how can I be dishonest as to my real feelings?", I point out that feelings are not the deciding factor. Bearing excruciating pain on the cross, Jesus cried, "Father, forgive them, for they do not know what they are doing" (Luke 23:34). It is quite possible, given the tormenting circumstances, that Jesus did not feel like forgiving (although not out of bitterness). But He called on the Father to forgive His executioners nevertheless.

Feelings don't determine forgiveness; God's Word does. We choose to forgive, because that's what God wants. But here is something amazing: When we choose to forgive, God cleanses our hearts of bitterness. When we honor God's Word by asking forgiveness for those who've wronged us, He not only forgives but changes our feelings from negative to positive.

Praying Prayers of Petition

In this section of the book I've tried to lay some biblical groundwork for making profession of God's

Word a regular part of our petitioning. The next part of the book gives some practical help in doing that. In it you will find a topical listing of selected promises along with sample petitions.

What will happen as you use these petitions? Well, your prayers will be received by Jesus who is the apostle and high priest of our profession (Hebrews 3:1). Then, Jesus, our priest and messenger ("apostle" means messenger) will relay our petitions to the Father. And since the Father delights in honoring His Word, our petitions, when based on His Word, are assured a response. As God says through Jeremiah, ". . . I am watching over my Word to perform it" (1:12).

Now if God is anxious to honor requests based on His Word, we should be anxious to make them. Of course, they should not only be for ourselves but for others too, because the Word not only gives "bread to the eater," but "seed to the sower" (Isa. 55:10)—that is, not only is it good for our own nourishment, but also for sowing good seed in others. But whether we pray for ourselves or for others, with Mary the mother of Jesus, our motto must ever be: "May it be as you have said" (Luke 1:38).

Remember, the words which fall from our lips have much power for good or evil. As Proverbs 18:21 puts it, "Death and life are in the power of the tongue." Thus, the Psalmist cautioned himself: "I will guard my ways, that I may not sin with my tongue" (39:1). However, the Psalmist also knows that good can come from his mouth, so he says: "The mouth of the righteous utters wisdom, and his tongue speaks justice" (37:30). And how does that come about? "The law (Word) of his God is in his heart" (v.31). That is how it should be as we pray and profess the promises in His Word.

So, as you consider these promises, I pray that the words of your mouth and the meditation of your heart (spirit) will be acceptable in God's sight (Ps. 19:14). And, indeed, if your requests are accompanied by and in agreement with the promises of His Word, they will be acceptable!

But you have to decide to do it. You need to make those daring decisions dictated by spiritual thinking. That takes backbone and resolve, but it is the way to activate God's power in your life, and when it is activated you will never be the same again.

I have a wise friend who shared the source of his wisdom in a prayer meeting not long ago. "I haven't shared this before," he said, "but for many years at my noontime meal I've asked God for wisdom." When he said that I immediately thought of James 1:5: "If any of you lacks wisdom, he should ask God, who gives generously to all without finding fault, and it will be given to him." I asked God on the spot to give me wisdom too, and I began to notice a marked difference in my counseling ministry. Professing James 1:5 and asking God for wisdom is now one of my daily prayers—one which God is answering.

God created us for His glory, but He doesn't receive glory when we're living in defeat. God never intended that we should live in defeat. As we profess His Word and act on it, He is glorified as He channels His power through us.

The passages of Scripture which follow are, as I've said, accompanied by appropriate prayers of petition. I believe they will help you learn to pray as I've been suggesting. But it should be clear that merely using these professions mechanically will not work ("vain repetitions," the Bible calls it). Such an approach will prove fruitless. We are not to come to God as a kind of grown-up's Santa Claus but as our heavenly Father. These prayers and professions should be simply a continuation of worship, of the thanksgiving and praise with which the Psalms encourage us to come into His presence.

Our heavenly Father knows when our motives are right. He knows whether we are out to glorify Him, or use Him for selfish gain. Be assured, He will not honor petitions brought for the latter reason. But when we come for kingdom purposes, and with right motives, He delights in honoring our requests.

When you meditate upon the Scriptures that follow, the Holy Spirit will show you how they apply to your friends' needs and to your own. He will lead you into prayer based upon them, which you will find to be one of the most exciting experiences of your life. Praying accompanied by the profession of these promises is exercising faith in the living power of the living Word. You will soon find yourself undergoing remarkable changes from the inside out, as, more and more, you become conformed to the image of God, exhibiting His characteristics in your life. No longer will you say, "Father, I hope to be . . .", but "Father, in Jesus Christ the living Word, I am!"

Access Into the Holy of Holies for Worship

Hebrews 10:19-22

Therefore, brothers, since we have confidence to enter the Most Holy Place by the blood of Jesus, by a new and living way opened for us through the curtain, that is, his body, and since we have a great priest over the house of God, let us draw near to God with a sincere heart in full assurance of faith, having our hearts sprinkled to cleanse us from a guilty conscience and having our bodies washed with pure water.

Profession in Prayer:
> Heavenly Father, according to Hebrews 10:19-22, through the blood of Jesus I can enter into your Holy of Holies, into your presence with full assurance. I am confident, I am clean, I am without fear, guilt, or condemnation.

Adequacy

2 Corinthians 3:4-6
> Such confidence as this is ours through Christ before God. Not that we are competent to claim anything for ourselves, but our competence comes from God. He has made us competent as ministers of a new covenant—not of the letter but of the Spirit; for the letter kills, but the Spirit gives life.

Profession in Prayer:
> Heavenly Father, according to 2 Corinthians 3:4-6, I have confidence toward you through Jesus Christ, and through Him you have made me adequate as a servant of the New Covenant.

Aging

A profession for the aging from Psalm 92

Psalm 92:13-15
> They are planted in the house of the Lord,
> they flourish in the courts of our God.
> They still bring forth fruit in old age,
> they are ever full of sap and green,
> to show that the Lord is upright;
> he is my rock, and there is no unrighteousness in him.

Alive

Romans 6:8-11
> Now if we died with Christ, we believe that we will

also live with him. For we know that since Christ was raised from the dead, he cannot die again; death no longer has mastery over him. The death he died, he died to sin once for all; but the life he lives, he lives to God. In the same way, count yourselves dead to sin but alive to God in Christ Jesus.

Profession in Prayer:
Heavenly Father, according to Romans 6:8-11, I am in Christ, identified with His death and resurrection. In Christ, I have died to sins once for all; I now live for you. I consider myself dead to sin, but alive to you in Christ Jesus.

Romans 6:22, 23
But now that you have been set free from sin and have become slaves to God, the benefit you reap leads to holiness, and the result is eternal life. For the wages of sin is death, but the gift of God is eternal life in Christ Jesus our Lord.

Profession in Prayer:
Heavenly Father, according to Romans 6:22, 23, I am a slave to Satan or to God. I choose to be your slave, knowing this will result in holiness and eternal life in your presence.

Romans 8:10
But if Christ is in you, your body is dead because of sin, yet your spirit is alive because of righteousness.

Profession in Prayer:
Heavenly Father, according to Romans 8:10, my

body is dead because of sin, but my spirit has been brought to life through the righteousness of Jesus Christ.

Romans 8:11
And if the Spirit of him who raised Jesus from the dead is living in you, he who raised Christ from the dead will also give life to your mortal bodies through his Spirit, who lives in you.

Profession in Prayer:
Heavenly Father, according to Romans 8:11, you are continually giving life to my mortal body through your Holy Spirit who dwells in me.

Galatians 2:20
I have been crucified with Christ and I no longer live, but Christ lives in me. The life I live in the body, I live by faith in the Son of God, who loved me and gave himself for me.

Profession in Prayer:
Heavenly Father, according to Galatians 2:20, I have been crucified with Christ, and I no longer live, but Christ lives in me; and the life that I now live in this body I live by the faith of your Son. My old desires have been nailed to the cross, and I receive the desires of my Lord, Jesus Christ.

Ephesians 2:4-6
But because of his great love for us, God, who is rich in mercy, made us alive with Christ even when we

were dead in transgressions—it is by grace you have been saved. And God raised us up with Christ and seated us with him in the heavenly realms in Christ Jesus.

Profession in Prayer:
Heavenly Father, according to Ephesians 2:4-6, you have made me alive with Christ. My spirit has been raised with Christ and seated at your right hand in Him; I am actually in your presence in the Most Holy Place in Christ.

---

1 Peter 1:23
For you have been born again, not of perishable seed, but of imperishable, through the living and enduring word of God.

Profession in Prayer:
Heavenly Father, according to 1 Peter 1:23, I have been born again through the imperishable, living and abiding Word of God, Jesus Christ. I will never die.

---

2 Peter 1:3
His divine power has given us everything we need for life and godliness through our knowledge of him who called us by his own glory and goodness.

Profession in Prayer:
Heavenly Father, according to 2 Peter 1:3, you have granted to me everything that I need relating to life and godliness. You have already made provision for

everything I need to live a godly and holy life, through a true, personal knowledge of your Son, Jesus. You have called me to your own glory and excellence through Jesus Christ.

---

1 John 2:23
No one who denies the Son has the Father; whoever acknowledges the Son has the Father also.

Profession in Prayer:
Heavenly Father, according to 1 John 2:23, since I confess Jesus Christ, your Son as Lord, I have you as my Father also, the Father of all life.

John 10:10
I have come that they may have life, and have it to the full.

Profession in Prayer:
Heavenly Father, according to John 10:10, Jesus came that I might have abundant, full and overflowing life. I know that He accomplished that for which He was sent, so I confess that in Him I do have abundant life.

Ambassadors

2 Corinthians 5:20
We are therefore Christ's ambassadors, as though God were making his appeal through us.

Profession in Prayer:
Heavenly Father, according to 2 Corinthians 5:20, I am an ambassador for Christ. You are entreating

the world through me as a part of the body of Christ. I am your agent here on earth. I am a vessel; you are the treasure.

Angels

1 Peter 3:21b, 22

. . . Jesus Christ, who has gone into heaven and is at God's right hand—with angels, authorities and powers in submission to him.

Profession in Prayer:

Heavenly Father, according to Hebrews 1:14, angels are ministering spirits sent to serve those who will inherit salvation. According to 1 Peter 3:21b, 22, since I am in Christ I can call upon angels to minister to the needs of members of the body of Christ. I have the authority in Christ over all the forces of darkness, who have been subjected to the authority of Christ.

Anger

Proverbs 16:32

He who is slow to anger is better than the mighty, and he who rules his spirit than he who takes a city.

Profession in Prayer:

Heavenly Father, according to Proverbs 16:32, it is good for me to be slow to anger and to have control of my spirit. Help me.

Romans 12:18-21

If it is possible, as far as it depends on you, live at peace with everyone. Do not take revenge, my friends, but leave room for God's wrath, for it is written: "It is mine to avenge; I will repay," says the Lord. On the contrary: "If your enemy is hungry, feed him; if he is thirsty, give him something to drink. In doing this, you will heap burning coals on his head." Do not be overcome by evil, but overcome evil with good.

Profession in Prayer:
Heavenly Father, according to Romans 12:18-21, I am to live at peace with everyone by not taking revenge. You will take care of revenge with your wrath. Instead I will do good. Therefore I will overcome evil.

Ephesians 4:26, 27
"In your anger do not sin": Do not let the sun go down while you are still angry, and do not give the devil a foothold.

Profession in Prayer:
Heavenly Father, according to Ephesians 4:26, 27, I will not end a day with anger toward another; therefore the devil will have no hold on me.

Colossians 3:7, 8
You used to walk in these ways, in the life you once lived. But now you must rid yourselves of all such things as these: anger, rage, malice, slander, and filthy language.

Profession in Prayer:
Heavenly Father, according to Colossins 3:7, 8, I am not to remain angry. I acknowledge my anger; I will

not attack another, but I will share with them my angry feelings. Then I can replace my anger with compassion, kindness, humility, gentleness, and patience. I receive these things through your Holy Spirit in me.

James 1:19, 20
My dear brothers, take note of this: Everyone should be quick to listen, slow to speak and slow to become angry, for man's anger does not bring about the righteous life that God desires.

Profession in Prayer:
Heavenly Father, following the instructions of James 1:19, 20, I will be quick to listen, slow to speak, and slow to become angry in order that your righteousness may flow through me.

Psalm 4:4
Be angry, but sin not; commune with your own hearts on your beds, and be silent.

Profession in Prayer:
Heavenly Father, according to Psalm 4:4, I will ponder in my quiet times the source of my anger. I will not sin.

Anxiety

Psalm 37:3, 4
Trust in the Lord, and do good; so you will dwell in the land, and enjoy security. Take delight in the Lord, and he will give you the desires of your heart.

Profession in Prayer:
> Heavenly Father, in Jesus I profess that Psalm 37, verses three and four are true for me. I am secure, I delight in you and the desires of my heart are being met.

Psalm 37:5, 6
> Commit your way to the Lord; trust in him, and he will act. He will bring forth your vindication as the light, and your right as the noonday.

Profession in Prayer:
> Heavenly Father, in Jesus I profess that Psalm 37, verses five and six are true for me. I am committing my way to you, I am trusting you. You will act. I am being delivered from anxiety and my face is beginning to shine like the noonday sun.

Matthew 6:25-27
> Therefore I tell you, do not worry about your life, what you will eat or drink; or about your body, what you will wear. Is not life more important than food, and the body more important than clothes? Look at the birds of the air; they do not sow or reap or store away in barns, and yet your heavenly Father feeds them. Are you not much more valuable than they? Who of you by worrying can add a single hour to his life?

Profession and Confession in Prayer:
> Heavenly Father, in Jesus I confess that I have worried and have been anxious. Please forgive me

for that. I receive your forgiveness. Father, my life is more important than the birds, and you take care of them. I profess that you will supply food and clothes for me too.

Matthew 6:31-34

So do not worry, saying, 'What shall we eat?' or 'What shall we drink?' or 'What shall we wear?' For the pagans run after all these things, and your heavenly Father knows that you need them. But seek first his kingdom and his righteousness, and all these things will be given to you as well. Therefore do not worry about tomorrow, for tomorrow will worry about itself. Each day has enough trouble of its own.

Profession and Confession in Prayer:
Heavenly Father, in Jesus I profess that Matthew 6:31-34 are true for me. I confess that I have been anxious and worried when I should have been exercising faith. I will seek first and foremost to build your kingdom by releasing your righteousness. Tomorrow will take care of itself, for it is in your hands.

Matthew 11:28-30

"Come to me, all you who are weary and burdened, and I will give you rest. Take my yoke upon you and learn from me, for I am gentle and humble in heart, and you will find rest for your souls. For my yoke is easy and my burden is light."

Profession in Prayer:
Heavenly Father, in Jesus I profess that Matthew 11:28-30 are true for me. I am coming to you with all my weariness and burdens. I cannot handle them alone. I am receiving your rest. Thank you, Father, for surrounding me with your gentle and loving Holy Spirit.

Romans 9:33
As it is written: "See, I lay in Zion a stone that causes men to stumble and a rock that makes them fall, and the one who trusts in him will never be put to shame [be shook up]."

Profession in Prayer:
I will never be put to shame, that is, shook up, in Christ. I will always be delighted in Him.

Philippians 4:6-8
Do not be anxious about anything, but in everything, by prayer and petition, with thanksgiving, present your requests to God. And the peace of God, which transcends all understanding, will guard your hearts and your minds in Christ Jesus.

Profession in Prayer:
Heavenly Father, according to Philippians 4:6-8, in Christ I am not anxious. I am receiving peace for each situation that could occur. And now I am receiving your peace which is greater than my intellect to guard my spirit and the sphere in which it dwells. Thank you.

Hebrews 13:5b, 6
> "Never will I leave you; never will I forsake you." So we say with confidence, "The Lord is my helper; I will not be afraid. What can man do to me?"

Profession in Prayer:
> Heavenly Father, according to Hebrews 13:5b, 6, in Christ I am not afraid. You are my helper, and you will never leave nor forsake me.

---

1 Peter 5:6, 7
> Humble yourselves, therefore, under God's mighty hand, that he may lift you up in due time. Cast all your anxiety on him because he cares for you.

Profession in Prayer:
> Heavenly Father, according to 1 Peter 5:6, 7, in Jesus I humble myself. You will lift me up in due time because you care for me. I put all my anxiety under the blood of Jesus.

Blessings

Galatians 3:7
> Understand, then, that those who believe are children of Abraham.

Galatians 3:9
> So those who have faith are blessed along with Abraham, the man of faith.

Galatians 3:13, 14
> Christ redeemed us from the curse of the law by becoming a curse for us, for it is written: "Cursed is everyone who is hung on a tree." He redeemed us in order

that the blessing given to Abraham might come to the Gentiles through Christ Jesus, so that by faith we might receive the promise of the Spirit.

Profession in Prayer:
Heavenly Father, according to Galatians 3:7, 9, and 13, in Christ I am a son (or daughter) of Abraham and am blessed with the blessing of Abraham; therefore, I thank you that Christ has redeemed me from the curse of the law, and I thank you that I have received the promised Holy Spirit through faithing into Christ Jesus.

Blood of Jesus

Ephesians 1:7
In him we have redemption through his blood, the forgiveness of sins, in accordance with the riches of God's grace that he lavished on us, with all wisdom and understanding.

Profession in Prayer:
Heavenly Father, according to Ephesians 1:7, through the blood of Jesus I am redeemed out of the hands of the devil.

---

1 John 1:7
But if we walk in the light, as he is in the light, we have fellowship with one another, and the blood of Jesus, his Son, [continually] purifies us from every sin.

Profession in Prayer:
Heavenly Father, according to 1 John 1:7, through the blood of Jesus I have fellowship with you, and the

blood of Jesus is continually cleansing me from all sin.

Romans 5:9
Since we have now been justified by his blood, how much more shall we be saved from God's wrath through him!

Profession in Prayer:
Heavenly Father, according to Romans 5:9, through the blood of Jesus I am justified, just-as-if-I'd-never-sinned.

Hebrews 9:14
How much more, then, will the blood of Christ, who through the eternal Spirit offered himself unblemished to God, cleanse our consciences from acts that lead to death, so that we may serve the living God!

Profession in Prayer:
Heavenly Father, according to Hebrews 9:14, through the blood of Jesus my conscience has been cleansed; Satan can no longer pound me from within with old failure and hurt. My conscience is cleansed!

---

1 Peter 1:18, 19
For you know that it was not with perishable things such as silver or gold that you were redeemed from the empty way of life handed down to you from your forefathers, but with the precious blood of Christ, a lamb without blemish or defect.

Profession in Prayer:
   Heavenly Father, according to 1 Peter 1:18, 19, I am delivered from the empty way of life I used to live.

Hebrews 10:19, 20
   Therefore, brothers, since we have confidence to enter the Most Holy Place by the blood of Jesus, by a new and living way opened for us through the curtain, that is, his body. . . .

Profession in Prayer:
   Heavenly Father, according to Hebrews 10:19, 20, I can enter into the presence of God without fear, guilt or condemnation.

Hebrews 13:12
   And so Jesus also suffered outside the city gate to make the people holy through his own blood.

Hebrews 13:15
   Through Jesus, therefore, let us continually offer to God a sacrifice of praise—the fruit of lips that confess his name.

Profession in Prayer:
   Heavenly Father, according to Hebrews 13:12, 15, through the blood of Jesus I have been sanctified, made holy, set apart for service. Not only that, through Jesus I can continually offer a sacrifice of praise!

---

1 Corinthians 6:19, 20
   Do you not know that your body is a temple of the

Holy Spirit, who is in you, whom you have received from God? You are not your own; you were bought at a price. Therefore honor God with your body.

Profession in Prayer:
Heavenly Father, according to 1 Corinthians 6:19, 20, through the blood of Jesus my body has become a temple of the Holy Spirit; therefore, Satan has no power over me and no part in me!

Colossians 1:19, 20
For God was pleased to have all his fullness dwell in him, and through him to reconcile to himself all things, whether things on earth or things in heaven, by making peace through his blood, shed on the cross.

Profession in Prayer:
Heavenly Father, according to Colossians 1:19, 20, through the blood of Jesus I have peace.

Buried With Christ

Romans 6:3, 4
Or don't you know that all of us who were baptized into Christ Jesus were baptized into his death? We were therefore buried with him through baptism into death in order that, just as Christ was raised from the dead through the glory of the Father, we too may live a new life.

Profession in Prayer:
Heavenly Father, according to Romans 6:3, 4, I have already been buried with Christ so that I may walk

in newness of life. My old nature has died with Christ, and I choose to walk in His new life according to your Word.

Characteristics of God

Romans 7:4
> So, my brothers, you also died to the law through the body of Christ, that you might belong to another, to him who was raised from the dead, in order that we might bear fruit to God.

Profession in Prayer:
> Heavenly Father, according to Romans 7:4, I have been joined to Christ; we are one with each other. I am teamed up, united with your omnipotence. You have done this so that I might bear fruit for you.

Romans 8:23
> Not only so, but we ourselves who have the firstfruits of the Spirit. . . .

Profession in Prayer:
> Heavenly Father, according to Romans 8:23, in Christ I have the firstfruits of the Spirit.

Galatians 5:22, 23
> But the fruit of the Spirit is love, joy, peace, patience, kindness, goodness, faithfulness, gentleness and self-control. Against such things there is no law.

Profession in Prayer:
> Heavenly Father, according to Galatians 5:22, 23, in

Christ I have the privilege of releasing the fruit of the Spirit, because you say that I received the Holy Spirit when I gave my life to you. I can choose to allow Holy Spirit fruit to control my life. I am filled with your love; I am a loving person. I am filled with your joy; I am joyful. I have your patience; I am patient. Your kindness flows through me; I am kind. You are faithful; in you I am faithful. I am filled with your goodness; I am good. Your gentleness fills me; I am gentle. My self is under the control of your Holy Spirit. I am no longer my own; I can allow your characteristics to flow through me in the power of the Spirit. I don't have to try to be these things, Father, because you say they are already there if I just let Christ live through me by the Spirit. I can rest in you through Christ while He lives through me. Thank you, Father.

Children of God

Romans 8:14

Those who are led by the Spirit of God are sons of God.

Profession in Prayer:

Heavenly Father, according to Romans 8:14, in Christ I am your son (or daughter). I can talk to you as my own Father, through Christ Jesus.

Romans 8:16, 17

The Spirit himself testifies with our spirit that we are God's children. Now if we are children, then we are heirs—heirs of God and co-heirs with Christ, if indeed we share in his sufferings in order that we may also share in his glory.

Profession in Prayer:
   Heavenly Father, according to Romans 8:16, 17, I am your child, and a joint-heir with Christ; all that belongs to Jesus is mine also, for your glory.

---

1 John 3:1
   How great is the love the Father has lavished on us, that we should be called children of God!

Profession in Prayer:
   Heavenly Father, according to 1 John 3:1, you have called me your child, and since you cannot lie, it is so.

Chosen

Ephesians 1:4
   For he chose us in him before the creation of the world to be holy and blameless in his sight.

Profession in Prayer:
   Heavenly Father, according to Ephesians 1:4, you have chosen me, in Christ, to be holy and blameless before you. I confess that I can only be that way as I abide in you.

---

1 Peter 2:9
   But you are a chosen people, a royal priesthood, a holy nation, a people belonging to God, that you may declare the praises of him who called you out of darkness into his wonderful light.

Profession in Prayer:
> Heavenly Father, according to 1 Peter 2:9, I am a part of a chosen people, a royal priesthood, a holy nation; I am a person for your own possession. In Christ, I am a high priest.

Cleansing From Sin

1 John 1:7
> But if we walk in the light, as he is in the light, we have fellowship with one another, and the blood of Jesus, his Son, purifies [continually cleanses] us from every sin.

Profession in Prayer:
> Heavenly Father, according to 1 John 1:7, through the blood of Jesus I have fellowship with you, and the blood of Jesus is continually cleansing me from all sin.

Complete

Colossians 2:10
> . . . and you have been given fullness in Christ, who is the head over every power and authority.

Profession in Prayer:
> Heavenly Father, according to Colossians 2:10, in Christ I have been made complete. Also, in Him I have authority over all principalities and powers of the darkness. You have put all things under Christ's feet (Eph. 1:22). No other powers can lord it over me as I abide in Him.

Confidence

Philippians 1:20
> I eagerly expect and hope that I will in no way be

ashamed, but will have sufficient courage so that now as always Christ will be exalted in my body, whether by life or by death.

Profession in Prayer:
Heavenly Father, according to Philippians 1:20, I can choose to exalt Christ as Lord of my body as long as I live. I make that spirit decision. Christ will always be on the throne of my life, for He alone is worthy to be exalted!

———

Philippians 1:6
Being confident of this, that he who began a good work in you will carry it on to completion until the day of Christ Jesus.

Profession in Prayer:
Heavenly Father, according to Philippians 1:6, I profess with the Apostle Paul that since you began a good work within me, you will carry it on to completion until the day of Christ Jesus.

Confusion

1 Corinthians 6:3
Do you not know that we will judge angels? How much more the things of this life!

Profession in Prayer:
Heavenly Father, according to 1 Corinthians 6:3, in Christ I have the ability to judge disputes in this life. I choose to desire your will only and trust you to show me the way.

1 Corinthians 6:12
> "Everything is permissible for me"—but not everything is beneficial. "Everything is permissible for me"—but I will not be mastered by anything.

Profession in Prayer:
> Heavenly Father, according to 1 Corinthians 6:12, in Christ I should not be mastered by anything. In Christ I am a master over all things; I understand this does not mean I can lord it over others, but that in Christ I do not have to let circumstances get me down.

Conscience—Inner Healing

Hebrews 9:14
> How much more, then, will the blood of Christ, who through the eternal Spirit offered himself unblemished to God, cleanse our consciences from acts that lead to death, so that we may serve the living God.

Profession in Prayer:
> Heavenly Father, according to Hebrews 9:14, through the blood of Jesus my conscience has been cleansed, and Satan can no longer pound me from within with old failure and hurt. My conscience is cleansed. Hallelujah!

Continually Saved

Romans 5:10, 11
> For if, when we were God's enemies, we were reconciled to him through the death of his Son, how

much more, having been reconciled, shall we be saved through his life! Not only is this so, but we also rejoice in God through our Lord Jesus Christ, through whom we have now received reconciliation.

Profession in Prayer:
Heavenly Father, according to Romans 5:10-11, I can rejoice in your presence through Jesus Christ because He has reconciled me to you; and because He lives in me, I shall be saved.

Correction—Chastening

Hebrews 12:10
Our fathers disciplined us for a little while as they thought best; but God disciplines us for our good, that we may share in his holiness.

Profession in Prayer:
Heavenly Father, according to Hebrews 12:10, I accept your discipline with joy, knowing that it is for my good, and through it I am able to continue to share in your holiness.

Criticism

Romans 14:13
Therefore, let us stop passing judgment on one another. Instead, make up your mind not to put any stumbling block or obstacle in your brother's way.

Profession in Prayer:
Heavenly Father, because Romans 14:13 forbids me to pass judgment on my brothers and sisters—because

this builds stumbling blocks for them—I will love them unconditionally instead. According to Galatians 5:22 I have an inexhaustible supply of your love for them.

Daily Strength

Psalm 68:19
Blessed be the Lord, who daily bears us up; God is our salvation.

Profession in Prayer:
Heavenly Father, according to Psalm 68:19, you daily give me strength, you bear me up, you are my salvation. I praise you.

Death

John 8:51
I tell you the truth, if a man keeps my word, he will never see death.

Profession in Prayer:
Heavenly Father, according to the words of Jesus in John 8:51, and since I am keeping your Word, I will never die; my spirit shall live forever in your presence.

Deliverance From Empty Ways of Life

1 Peter 1:18, 19
For you know that it was not with perishable things such as silver or gold that you were redeemed from the empty way of life handed down to you from your

forefathers, but with the precious blood of Christ, a lamb without blemish or defect.

Profession in Prayer:
Heavenly Father, according to 1 Peter 1:18, 19, through the blood of Jesus I have been redeemed from the empty way of life I used to live. Glory!

Delivered

Romans 6:6, 7
For we know that our old self was crucified with him so that the body of sin might be rendered powerless, that we should no longer be slaves to sin—because anyone who has died has been freed from sin.

Profession in Prayer:
Heavenly Father, according to Romans 6:6, 7, because my old self has been crucified with Christ, my body of sin has been done away with and I am freed from the control of sin. Thank you for freedom.

Depression

Psalm 43:5
Why are you cast down, O my soul, and why are you disquieted within me? Hope in God; for I shall again praise him, my help and my God.

Profession in Prayer:
Heavenly Father, I ask myself the same questions as the Psalmist. I do hope in you, I do praise you. You are my help, O God.

Isaiah 41:10
. . . fear not, for I am with you, be not dismayed, for

I am your God; I will strengthen you, I will help you, I will uphold you with my victorious right hand.

Profession in Prayer:
Heavenly Father, according to Isaiah 41:10, in Jesus I am not afraid or depressed because you are my God and you are with me. You are strengthening me, helping me, and holding me up with your hands of victory. Thank you.

Philippians 4:8
Finally, brothers, whatever is true, whatever is noble, whatever is right, whatever is pure, whatever is lovely, whatever is admirable—if anything is excellent or praiseworthy—think about such things.

Profession in Prayer:
Father, in obedience to Philippians 4:8, I am thinking about true, noble, right, pure, lovely, admirable, excellent, and praiseworthy things.

Divine Nature

2 Peter 1:4
Through these he has given us his very great and precious promises, so that through them you may participate in the divine nature and escape the corruption in the world caused by evil desires.

Profession in Prayer:
Heavenly Father, according to 2 Peter 1:4, in Christ I am a partaker of your divine nature and have escaped the corruption that is in the world by evil

desires. Through Jesus Christ your own divine nature is flowing through my life as I rest in Jesus.

Drawing Power

2 Corinthians 9:14
And in their prayers for you their hearts will go out to you, because of the surpassing grace God has given you.

Profession in Prayer:
Heavenly Father, according to 2 Corinthians 9:14, as I allow your surpassing grace to flow through me, people are attracted to your presence flowing through me. Hallelujah!

Dwelling Place of God

1 Corinthians 3:16
Don't you know that you yourselves are God's temple and that God's Spirit lives in you?

Profession in Prayer:
Heavenly Father, according to 1 Corinthians 3:16, I am your temple. You, the almighty Creator of the universe, dwell in me by your Spirit! I praise you for this wonderful reality. Help me to always be conscious of this glorious fact. I am no longer merely a mortal being. I am inhabited by you!

---

1 Corinthians 6:13b
The body is not meant for sexual immorality, but for the Lord, and the Lord for the body.

Profession in Prayer:
Heavenly Father, according to 1 Corinthians 6:13b, since I am your temple I can no longer treat my body as if it were mine. My body is now for you and for your glory, not for immorality. I know that you will help me take care of it, since it is yours.

---

1 Corinthians 6:19, 20
Do you not know that your body is a temple of the Holy Spirit, who is in you, whom you have received from God? You are not your own; you were bought at a price. Therefore honor God with your body.

Profession in Prayer:
Heavenly Father, according to 1 Corinthians 6:19, 20, this body that I live in is a temple of the Holy Spirit. My spirit is united with your Holy Spirit. The price I pay to become a temple for your Holy Spirit is this: I no longer own my body. This means I will do things according to your will. I have traded my desires for your desire. Father, I choose to glorify you while I am in this body.

Energized

Philippians 2:13
. . . For it is God who works in you to will and to act according to his good purpose.

Profession in Prayer:
Heavenly Father, according to Philippians 2:13, as I abide in Christ, you work in me, making your will my own, then energizing me with your ability so I can do your good pleasure. Glory!

Philippians 4:13
I can do everything through him who gives me strength.

Profession in Prayer:
Heavenly Father, according to Philippians 4:13, I can do everything you want me to do through Christ, who is my strength.

Eternal Life

1 John 5:13
I write these things to you who believe in the name of the Son of God so that you may know that you have eternal life.

Profession in Prayer:
Heavenly Father, according to 1 John 5:13, in Christ I have eternal life. I understand that in Him I have life eternal right now!

---

1 Corinthians 15:54, 55
When the perishable has been clothed with the imperishable, and the mortal with immortality, then the saying that is written will come true: "Death has been swallowed up in victory." "Where, O death, is your victory? Where, O death, is your sting?"

Profession in Prayer:
Heavenly Father, according to 1 Corinthians 15:54, 55, when my physical body dies I will become clothed with immortality. In Christ I need not fear

death; indeed, I look forward to death as the gateway to living forever in your glorious presence.

Faithing

Romans 4:23, 24
> The words "it was credited to him" were written not for him alone, but also for us, to whom God will credit righteousness—for us who believe in him who raised Jesus our Lord from the dead.

Profession in Prayer:
> Heavenly Father, according to Romans 4:23, 24, as I continue to exercise faith into you, the One who raised Jesus my Lord from the dead, you will continue to profess *(logos)* or send righteousness into and through me.

Failure

Philippians 3:12-14
> Not that I have already obtained all this, or have already been made perfect, but I press on to take hold of that for which Christ Jesus took hold of me. Brothers, I do not consider myself yet to have taken hold of it. But one thing I do: Forgetting what is behind and straining toward what is ahead, I press toward the goal to win the prize for which God has called me heavenward in Christ Jesus.

Profession in Prayer:
> Heavenly Father, Philippians 3:12-14 is my profession too. I have often failed, but I am forgiven. I am not yet perfect, but I am pressing on toward that

heavenly goal. Forgetting the things that are behind makes me thankful that Christ Jesus took hold of me and gave me an eternal destiny.

Family of God

Ephesians 2:19
Consequently, you are no longer foreigners and aliens, but fellow citizens with God's people and members of God's household.

Profession in Prayer:
Heavenly Father, according to Ephesians 2:19, in Christ I am a fellow citizen with the saints, and am a member of your household. I understand that I am to treat my brothers and sisters in Christ as fellow members of your family!

Fear

1 John 4:18
There is no fear in love. But perfect love drives out fear, because fear has to do with punishment.

Profession in Prayer:
Heavenly Father, according to 1 John 4:18, there is no fear in love. Since I am abiding in your love I need not fear. What can man or Satan do to me? Father, I am convinced that nothing can keep me from your love; what else is there to fear?

Psalm 27:1 is a profession:
The Lord is my light and my salvation; whom shall I

fear? The Lord is the stronghold of my life; of whom shall I be afraid?

Psalm 46:1, 2a is a profession:
God is our refuge and strength, a very present help in trouble. Therefore we will not fear though the earth should change. . . .

Fellowship With God

1 John 1:3
We proclaim to you what we have seen and heard, so that you also may have fellowship with us. And our fellowship is with the Father and with his Son, Jesus Christ.

Profession in Prayer:
Heavenly Father, according to 1 John 1:3, through Jesus Christ I can have fellowship with you. I can commune with you, the Creator and Sustainer of this universe.

---

1 John 1:7
But if we walk in the light, as he is in the light, we have fellowship with one another, and the blood of Jesus, his Son, [continually] purifies us from every sin.

Profession in Prayer:
Heavenly Father, according to 1 John 1:7, through the blood of Jesus I have fellowship with you; and the blood of Jesus, your Son, continually purifies me from all unknown sin.

Finances

Hebrews 13:5-7
> Keep your lives free from the love of money and be content with what you have, because God has said, "Never will I leave you; never will I forsake you." So we say with confidence, "The Lord is my helper; I will not be afraid. What can man do to me?"

Profession in Prayer:
> Heavenly Father, since you have promised in Hebrews 13:5-7 that you will never leave or forsake me, that you will be my helper, I need not be afraid regarding my finances. I am content.

Forgiven

Colossians 2:13, 14
> When you were dead in your sins and in the uncircumcision of your sinful nature, God made you alive with Christ. He forgave us all our sins, having canceled the written code, with its regulations, that was against us and that stood opposed to us; he took it away, nailing it to the cross.

Profession in Prayer:
> Heavenly Father, according to Colossians 2:13 and 14, you have made me alive together with Christ Jesus, and all my sins are forgiven. My certificate of debt, my sinful nature, has been cancelled and taken out of the way. Christ's work has freed me that I may bring glory to you, heavenly Father!

Forgiving Others

Proverbs 17:9
> He who forgives an offense seeks love, but he who repeats a matter alienates a friend.

Profession in Prayer:
Heavenly Father, according to Proverbs 17:9, love can be mine by granting forgiveness. I will seek love and not alienation.

Freedom

Romans 8:12
Therefore, brothers, we have an obligation—but it is not to our sinful nature, to live according to it.

Profession in Prayer:
Heavenly Father, according to Romans 8:12, through Jesus I am no longer under obligation to live according to my flesh. It has been crucified with Jesus, and I am free to live according to the Holy Spirit who is within me.

Galatians 5:1
It is for freedom that Christ has set us free. Stand firm, then, and do not let yourselves be burdened again by a yoke of slavery.

Profession in Prayer:
Heavenly Father, according to Galatians 5:1, Christ has set me free; I will never subject myself again to a yoke of slavery to sin.

John 8:36
So if the Son sets you free, you will be free indeed.

Profession in Prayer:
Heavenly Father, according to the words of Jesus in

John 8:36, Christ has set me free. I am truly free to be all that you intended when you created me. Hallelujah!

Freedom From Oppression—Security

Psalm 17:1-5

Hear a just cause, O Lord; attend to my cry! Give ear to my prayer from lips free of deceit! From thee let my vindication come! Let thy eyes see the right! If thou triest my heart, if thou visitest me by night, if thou testest me, thou wilt find no wickedness in me; my mouth does not transgress. With regard to the works of men, by the word of thy lips I have avoided the ways of the violent. My steps have held fast to thy paths, my feet have not slipped.

Profession in Prayer:

Heavenly Father, according to Psalm 17:1-5, I ask you to search me, day or night. I profess that by your Word, I too am avoiding the ways of the violent. My steps shall be in the path of righteousness. I shall not slip.

Freedom From Sin

1 John 5:18

We know that anyone born of God does not continue to sin; the one who was born of God keeps him safe, and the evil one does not touch him.

Profession in Prayer:

Heavenly Father, according to 1 John 5:18, since I am born again, I do not need to continue the practice of sinning willfully. I will not. I am safe from Satan's power; he cannot even touch me.

Fruit Bearing

John 15:5
> I am the vine; you are the branches. If a man remains in me and I in him, he will bear much fruit; apart from me you can do nothing.

Profession in Prayer:
> Heavenly Father, according to John 15:4, you are the vine and I am a branch. Therefore, I have much fruit, or your characteristics, flowing in and through me! Without you I could do nothing.

Gladness

1 Chronicles 29:11-13   David's Profession
> Thine, O Lord, is the greatness, and the power, and the glory, and the victory, and the majesty; for all that is in the heavens and in the earth is thine; thine is the kingdom, O Lord, and thou art exalted as head above all. Both riches and honor come from thee, and thou rulest over all. In thy hand are power and might; and in thy hand it is to make great and to give strength to all. And now we thank thee, our God, and praise thy glorious name.

Philippians 1:20   Paul's Profession
> I eagerly expect and hope that I will in no way be ashamed, but will have sufficient courage so that now as always Christ will be exalted in my body, whether by life or by death.

Good Works

Ephesians 2:10
> For we are God's workmanship, created in Christ

Jesus to do good works, which God prepared in advance for us to do.

Profession in Prayer:
Heavenly Father, according to Ephesians 2:10, I am your workmanship in Christ. Before I was born you prepared good works for me to do in Christ. That is why I remain in this physical body—to bring glory to you by doing the things you have prepared for me in Christ. I confess I could not do these things without your Holy Spirit within me.

Guidance

Psalm 25:10
All the paths of the Lord are steadfast love and faithfulness, for those who keep his covenant and his testimonies.

Profession in Prayer:
Heavenly Father, according to Psalm 25:10, as I honor the new faithing covenant and follow your Word, my paths shall be within your steadfast love and faithfulness.

Psalm 25:12
Who is the man that fears the Lord? Him will he instruct in the way that he should choose.

Profession in Prayer:
Heavenly Father, according to Psalm 25:12, as I stand before you in awe and astonishment, you have promised to instruct me in the way I should make choices and decisions, and I choose to receive your instructions.

Proverbs 16:9
A man's mind plans his way, but the Lord directs his steps.

Profession in Prayer:
Heavenly Father, according to Proverbs 16:9, you are greater than my thinking—you are directing my steps. Praise your high and holy name!

Proverbs 16:1-3
The plans of the mind belong to man, but the answer of the tongue is from the Lord. All the ways of a man are pure in his own eyes, but the Lord weighs the spirit. Commit your work to the Lord, and your plans will be established.

Profession in Prayer:
Heavenly Father, according to Proverbs 16:1-3, as I commit my work unto you, my plans shall be established. Weigh my spirit, search me—then direct me. Thank you.

Proverbs 3:5, 6
Trust in the Lord with all your heart [spirit], and do not rely on your own insight. In all your ways acknowledge him, and he will make straight your paths.

Profession in Prayer:
Heavenly Father, according to Proverbs 3:5 and 6, as I exercise faith into you with my spirit decisions and lean not upon my intellectual reasonings, you will guide me.

Psalm 32:8, 9
> I will instruct you and teach you the way you should go; I will counsel you with my eye upon you. Be not like a horse or a mule, without understanding, which must be curbed with bit and bridle, else it will not keep with you.

Profession in Prayer:
> Heavenly Father, according to Psalm 32:8 and 9, I open my spirit to you for instruction. You are keeping your eye upon me, helping me not to be hardheaded and stubborn as a mule. Keep me easy to lead, Father.

Healing

Isaiah 53:4, 5
> Surely He has borne our griefs [sicknesses] and carried our sorrows [pains]; yet we esteemed him stricken, smitten by God, and afflicted. But he was wounded for our transgressions, he was bruised for our iniquities; upon him was the chastisement that made us whole, and with his stripes we are healed.

Profession in Prayer:
> Heavenly Father, according to Isaiah 53:4 and 5, Jesus bore our griefs, sorrows, sicknesses, and pains on the cross. By His stripes I am healed.

Matthew 8:16, 17
> When evening came, many who were demon-possessed were brought to him, and he drove out the spirits with a word and healed all the sick. This was to

fulfill what was spoken through the prophet Isaiah: "He took up our infirmities and carried our diseases."

Profession in Prayer:
Heavenly Father, according to Matthew 8:16, 17, through Jesus my diseases and illnesses are healed. Bring about the evidence in your way, in your time. Your delay is not your denial. I am being healed.

---

1 Peter 2:24
He himself bore our sins in his body on the tree, so that we might die to sins and live for righteousness; by his wounds you have been healed.

Profession in Prayer:
Heavenly Father, according to 1 Peter 2:24, through Jesus Christ I am healed. Sickness cannot lord it over me. Thank you that you take care of your temple, my body. I understand there may be times of testing to reveal your glory, but your delay is not your denial.

Help in Testing

1 Corinthians 10:13
No temptation has seized you except what is common to man. And God is faithful; he will not let you be tempted beyond what you can bear. But when you are tempted, he will also provide a way out so that you can stand up under it.

Profession in Prayer:
Heavenly Father, according to 1 Corinthians 10:13,

I will never be tempted so strongly that I must fail. You may test me beyond my fleshly strength, but you will never test me beyond my resources, which are your Holy Spirit and His characteristics and gifts. I can be victorious in any test that you allow to come upon me. Praise your holy name!

Hebrews 4:14-16
Therefore, since we have a great high priest who has gone through the heavens, Jesus the Son of God, let us hold firmly to the faith we profess. For we do not have a high priest who is unable to sympathize with our weaknesses, but we have one who has been tempted in every way, just as we are—yet was without sin. Let us then approach the throne of grace with confidence, so that we may receive mercy and find grace to help us in our time of need.

Profession in Prayer:
Heavenly Father, according to Hebrews 4:14-16, I have my high priest, Jesus. He understands and sympathizes with me in my weaknesses. I profess that I am coming to your throne with confidence to receive mercy, grace, and help. In fact I am receiving help right now.

Holy Spirit

Romans 7:6
But now, by dying to what once bound us, we have been released from the law so that we serve in the new way of the Spirit, and not in the old way of the written code.

Profession in Prayer:
> Heavenly Father, according to Roman 7:6, I have been released from the law to serve in the newness of the Holy Spirit.

---

1 Corinthians 2:12
> We have not received the spirit of the world but the Spirit who is from God, that we may understand what God has freely given us.

Profession in Prayer:
> Heavenly Father, according to 1 Corinthians 2:12, I have received the Holy Spirit from you in order that I might know the things you freely give me.

Titus 3:5, 6
> . . . He saved us, not because of righteous things we had done, but because of his mercy. He saved us through the washing of rebirth and renewal by the Holy Spirit, whom he poured out on us generously through Jesus Christ our Savior.

Profession in Prayer:
> Heavenly Father, according to Titus 3:5, 6, I have been saved according to your mercy, by the washing away of my old sinful nature and replacing it with the nature of Christ. Your Holy Spirit has renewed my mind also; I am acceptable in Christ. Your Holy Spirit has been richly poured out upon me through Jesus Christ, my Savior. I don't need to always feel it; your Word says it is so, therefore I receive it as truth.

Galatians 3:13, 14b
Christ redeemed us from the curse of the law by becoming a curse for us, for it is written: "Cursed is everyone who is hung on a tree." He redeemed us in order that the blessing given to Abraham might come to the Gentiles through Christ Jesus, so that by faith we might receive the promise of the Spirit.

Profession in Prayer:
Heavenly Father, according to Galatians 3:13, 14b Christ has redeemed me from the curse of the law in order that I might receive the promise of Abraham through faith—the Holy Spirit. I receive Him as an Honored Guest in my life.

Galatians 5:16
So I say, live by the Spirit, and you will not gratify the desires of the sinful nature.

Profession in Prayer:
Heavenly Father, according to Galatians 5:16, I make a spirit decision to walk by your Holy Spirit, not by my flesh. I will walk according to the ability of Christ within me.

Ephesians 1:13, 14
And you also were included in Christ when you heard the word of truth, the gospel of your salvation. Having believed, you were marked in him with a seal, the promised Holy Spirit, who is a deposit guaranteeing our inheritance until the redemption of those who are God's possession—to the praise of his glory.

Profession in Prayer:
> Heavenly Father, according to Ephesians 1:13, 14, I have been sealed in Christ with the Holy Spirit, and I am your possession, to the praise of your glory.

Insults

Matthew 5:11, 12
> "Blessed are you when people insult you, persecute you and falsely say all kinds of evil against you because of me. Rejoice and be glad, because great is your reward in heaven, for in the same way they persecuted the prophets who were before you.

Profession in Prayer:
> Heavenly Father, according to Matthew 5:11, 12, I place myself in your care, knowing that if people insult me and persecute me because of my Lord Jesus, I am blessed; and my reward in heaven will be great.

---

1 Peter 4:14
> If you are insulted because of the name of Christ, you are blessed, for the Spirit of glory and of God rests on you.

Profession in Prayer:
> Heavenly Father, according to 1 Peter 4:14, since I am being insulted for bearing your name, I am being blessed. It doesn't feel like I am being blessed, but I receive blessing because your Word says so.

Jesus

1 Peter 1:21
> Through him you believe in God, who raised him

from the dead and glorified him, and so your faith and hope are in God.

Profession in Prayer:
Heavenly Father, according to 1 Peter 1:21, I have the privilege to exercise faith through Jesus into you. You are receiving my faithing and hope. Thanks and praise be to Jesus and to you, Father.

Joy

Galatians 5:22
But the fruit of the Spirit is love, joy. . . .

Profession in Prayer:
Heavenly Father, according to Galatians 5:22, one of the fruits of the Holy Spirit within me is joy; I receive this joy for myself. As this joy blesses me I will be joy to others as your fragrance of joy flows through me. Thank you.

Justification—
Just-As-If-I'd-Never-Sinned

Romans 5:9
Since we have now been justified by his blood, how much more shall we be saved from God's wrath through him!

Profession in Prayer:
Heavenly Father, according to Romans 5:9, through the blood of Jesus I am justified, just-as-if-I'd-never-sinned.

Romans 3:28
For we maintain that a man is justified by faith apart

from observing the law.

Profession in Prayer:
Heavenly Father, according to Romans 3:28, through Jesus Christ I have been justified by faithing apart from the works of the law.

Laziness

Hebrews 6:12
We do not want you to become lazy, but to imitate those who through faith and patience inherit what has been promised.

Profession in Prayer:
Heavenly Father, according to Hebrews 6:12, through faithing and patience I will inherit the promises. I will not become lazy and fail to exercise faith and act upon the promises.

Liberty

2 Corinthians 3:17
Now the Lord is the Spirit, and where the Spirit of the Lord is, there is freedom.

Profession in Prayer:
Heavenly Father, according to 2 Corinthians 3:17, your Holy Spirit has set me free.

Life by Profession of the Mouth

Proverbs 18:20, 21
From the fruit of his mouth a man is satisfied; he is satisfied by the yield of his lips. Death and life are in

the power of the tongue, and those who love it will eat its fruits.

Profession in Prayer:
Heavenly Father, according to Proverbs 18:20, 21, by professing your Word with my mouth I am speaking life words. I love to profess, Father, for it satisfies my innermost needs.

Love

Romans 5:5
And hope does not disappoint us, because God has poured out his love into our hearts by the Holy Spirit, whom he has given us.

Profession in Prayer:
Heavenly Father, according to Romans 5:5, your love has indeed been poured out into my spirit through your Holy Spirit who has been given me. Your perfect love flows through my spirit into the world around me. People can experience your love through me.

---

2 Corinthians 5:14
For Christ's love compels us, because we are convinced that one died for all, and therefore all died.

Profession in Prayer:
Heavenly Father, according to 2 Corinthians 5:14, I am controlled by the love of Jesus Christ. My actions are love actions.

---

2 Timothy 1:7
For God did not give us a spirit of timidity, but a

spirit of power, of love and self-discipline.

Profession in Prayer:
Heavenly Father, according to 2 Timothy 1:7, I do not have a spirit of timidity or fear. I have Holy Spirit ability: love, power, and a sound mind—sound because it has been renewed, or adjusted, by the Word of God.

---

1 John 2:10
Whoever loves his brother lives in the light, and there is nothing in him to make him stumble.

Profession in Prayer:
Heavenly Father, according 1 John 2:10, the love of God is in me; I love all men. Therefore I am abiding in the light, and there is nothing in me to make me stumble.

---

1 Corinthians 13:4-8a
Love is patient, love is kind. It does not envy, it does not boast, it is not proud. It is not rude, it is not self-seeking, it is not easily angered, it keeps no record of wrongs. Love does not delight in evil but rejoices with the truth. It always protects, always trusts, always hopes, always perseveres. Love never fails.

Profession in Prayer:
Heavenly Father, according to Galatians 5:22, love is a characteristic of your Spirit in me; therefore according to 1 Corinthians 13:4-8a, I am patient,

kind, not envious, not boastful, and I am not proud in the wrong sense. I am not rude, not self-seeking, easily angered, and I keep no record of other persons' wrongs or failings. I will always protect, trust, hope, and persevere. Your love in me and through me will never fail.

Galatians 5:22a
But the fruit of the Spirit is love. . . .

Profession in Prayer:
Heavenly Father, according to Galatians 5:22a, one of the characteristics of your Holy Spirit living within me is love. When my human love fails I will love with your divine, never-ending love continually.

---

1 John 4:7, 8
Dear friends, let us love one another, for love comes from God. Everyone who loves has been born of God and knows God. Whoever does not love does not know God, because God is love.

Profession in Prayer:
Heavenly Father, according to 1 John 4:7, 8, you are love. I am in Christ in you; therefore I am a lover.

Romans 5:5
And hope does not disappoint us, because God has poured out his love into our hearts by the Holy Spirit, whom he has given us.

Profession in Prayer:
   Heavenly Father, according to Romans 5:5, you have given me divine love by means of the Holy Spirit in me. Therefore I can love with divine love.

Mind (Sphere) of Christ

1 Corinthians 2:16
   "For who has known the mind of the Lord that he may instruct him?" But we have the mind of Christ.

Profession in Prayer:
   Heavenly Father, according to 1 Corinthians 2:16, I have the mind of Christ. I *have* the mind of Christ. I am operating in the sphere of Christ.

Mind, Sphere, *Nous*—Renewed

Romans 12:1, 2
   Therefore, I urge you, brothers, in view of God's mercy, to offer your bodies as living sacrifices, holy and pleasing to God—which is your spiritual worship. Do not conform any longer to the pattern of this world, but be transformed by the renewing of your mind. Then you will be able to test and approve what God's will is—his good, pleasing and perfect will.

Profession in Prayer:
   Heavenly Father, according to Romans 12:1, 2, I am to offer myself to you as a living sacrifice; I do it now. I will no longer depend upon my intellect and seek self-praise as the world does. I am now being transformed by the renewing of my mind, the sphere in which my spirit lives. Now I can test and approve what your good, pleasing and perfect will is! Praise your name.

Needs

2 Corinthians 9:8
>And God is able to make all grace abound to you, so that in all things at all times, having all that you need, you will abound in every good work.

Profession in Prayer:
>Heavenly Father, according to 2 Corinthians 9:8, God is my Father; therefore I always have all that I need in every situation I encounter, plus I have abundance to give on every occasion.

Philippians 4:19
>And my God will meet all your needs according to his glorious riches in Christ Jesus.

Profession in Prayer:
>Heavenly Father, according to Philippians 4:19, God, my Father, will supply all my future needs. He has supplied all my past needs; He is supplying all my present needs. He is my sufficiency!

Hebrews 4:16
>Let us then approach the throne of grace with confidence, so that we may receive mercy and find grace to help us in our time of need.

Profession in Prayer:
>Heavenly Father, according to Hebrews 4:16, as I approach your throne in my time of need, you give me mercy and grace. I receive it.

New Beginning

2 Corinthians 5:17
> Therefore, if anyone is in Christ, he is a new creation; the old has gone, the new has come!

Profession in Prayer:
> Heavenly Father, according to 2 Corinthians 5:17, I am a new creation. My past has been forgiven and erased; I have a totally new beginning.

New Creation

Ephesians 4:22-24
> You were taught, with regard to your former way of life, to put off your old self, which is being corrupted by its deceitful desires; to be made new in the attitude of your minds; and to put on the new self, created to be like God in true righteousness and holiness.

Profession in Prayer:
> Heavenly Father, according to Ephesians 4:22-24, in Christ my old nature has been crucified; I choose to lay it aside and be renewed in the spirit of my mind (sphere). According to your command, I put on the new self in Christ, which is in your likeness and has been created in righteousness and holiness. I am a new creation, righteous and holy in Christ! To you be all the glory!

Patience

James 5:7, 8
> Be patient, then, brothers, until the Lord's coming.

See how the farmer waits for the land to yield its valuable crop and how patient he is for the fall and spring rains. You too, be patient and stand firm, because the Lord's coming is near.

Profession in Prayer:
Heavenly Father, according to James 5:7, 8, I can be patient. I am patient because you command it and because you supply patience as fruit of your Spirit, who dwells within me.

Galatians 5:22, 23a
But the fruit of the Spirit is love, joy, peace, *patience*, kindness, goodness, faithfulness, gentleness and self-control. [Italics mine]

Profession in Prayer:
Heavenly Father, according to Galatians 5:22, 23a, I have your divine enabling of patience within me. Therefore, I will be patient and exude patience toward others today. Thank you for patience.

Galatians 6:9
Let us not become weary in doing good, for at the proper time we will reap a harvest if we do not give up.

Profession in Prayer:
Heavenly Father, according to Galatians 6:9, I am not to become weary or impatient while doing good. Therefore, at the proper time I will reap a harvest of benefit.

Peace

Colossians 1:19, 20
> For God was pleased to have all his fullness dwell in him, and through him to reconcile to himself all things, whether things on earth or things in heaven, by making peace through his blood, shed on the cross.

Profession in Prayer:
> Heavenly Father, according to Colossians 1:19, 20, through the blood of Jesus I have peace.

Romans 5:1
> Therefore, since we have been justified through faith, we have peace with God through our Lord Jesus Christ.

Profession in Prayer:
> Heavenly Father, according to Romans 5:1, through Jesus Christ I have peace.

Ephesians 2:13, 14a
> But now in Christ Jesus you who once were far away have been brought near through the blood of Christ. For he himself is our peace. . . .

Profession in Prayer:
> Heavenly Father, according to Ephesians 2:13, 14a, by the blood of Jesus, I have been brought near to the Father—that is, into His presence. Jesus is my peace with God.

Galatians 5:22
> But the fruit of the Spirit is love, joy, peace. . . .

Profession in Prayer:
Heavenly Father, according to Galatians 5:22, peace, a characteristic of the Holy Spirit, is within me. I release your peace to radiate in and through me. Father, in Jesus, I am peace.

Colossians 3:15
Let the peace of Christ rule in your hearts, since, as members of one body, you were called to peace. And be thankful.

Profession in Prayer:
Heavenly Father, according to Colossians 3:15, you have called me to peace. By your Spirit I choose to let the peace of Christ Jesus rule in my spirit.

Peacemakers

James 3:18
Peacemakers who sow in peace raise a harvest of righteousness.

Profession in Prayer:
Heavenly Father, according to James 3:18, as I sow in peace I will raise a harvest of righteousness. I have your Spirit characteristic called peace within me. Right now I am releasing it to bring forth a rich harvest of righteousness.

Romans 8:15
For you did not receive a spirit that makes you a slave again to fear, but you received the Spirit of

sonship. And by him we cry, "Abba, Father."

Profession in Prayer:
Heavenly Father, according to Romans 8:15, I have not received a spirit of slavery leading to fear; I have received a spirit of adoption as a son by which I can say, "Abba, Father," to you, God almighty. You are more than enough.

Perfect Before the Father

Hebrews 10:10 and 14
And by that will, we have been made holy through the sacrifice of the body of Jesus Christ once for all . . . because by one sacrifice he has made perfect forever those who are being made holy.

Profession in Prayer:
Heavenly Father, according to Hebrews 10:10 and 14, by your will I have been made holy through the sacrifice of Jesus' blood—once and forever. Even though you are continually drawing me toward the holy life, I still at times fail; yet you see me as perfect through the blood of Jesus. Praise be unto Jesus for His marvelous gift to me of His shed blood.

Possibilities

Matthew 17:20b, 21
". . . If you have faith as small as a mustard seed, you can say to this mountain, 'Move from here to there' and it will move. Nothing will be impossible for you."

Profession in Prayer:
Heavenly Father, according to Matthew 17:20b, 21 since I am exercising faith, nothing will be impossible that you call me to do.

Mark 9:23b
"Everything is possible for him who believes."

Profession in Prayer:
Heavenly Father, according to Mark 9:23b, nothing is impossible for me if I exercise faith. My intellect simply cannot comprehend that, but I receive it as a fact since your Word says so.

Luke 18:27
Jesus replied, "What is impossible with men is possible with God."

Profession in Prayer:
Heavenly Father, thanks for Luke 18:27; that verse makes it easier for me to exercise faith.

Praise Professions

Psalm 7:17
I will give the Lord the thanks due to his righteousness, and I will sing praise to the name of the Lord, the Most High.

Psalm 9:1, 2
I will give thanks to the Lord with my whole heart;
I will tell of all thy wonderful deeds.
I will be glad and exult in thee,
I will sing praise to thy name, O Most High.

Pride

Romans 12:6-8
We have different gifts, according to the grace given

us. If a man's gift is prophesying, let him use it in proportion to his faith. If it is serving, let him serve; if it is teaching, let him teach; if it is encouraging, let him encourage; if it is contributing to the needs of others, let him give generously; if it is leadership, let him govern diligently; if it is showing mercy, let him do it cheerfully.

Profession in Prayer:
Heavenly Father, according to Romans 12:6-8, I am not to be proud concerning the gift you have given me. I profess that I will not be proud, but I will make your gift available for the upbuilding of the kingdom today, cheerfully.

Profession

Psalm 37:30, 31
The mouth of the righteous utters wisdom, and his tongue speaks justice. The law of his God is in his heart; his steps do not slip.

Profession in Prayer:
Heavenly Father, according to Psalm 37:30 and 31, my mouth utters wisdom and justice. Your Word is in my spirit, therefore my feet will not slip. I am secure.

Profession, Evil

Psalm 39:1
I said, "I will guard my ways, that I may not sin with my tongue."

Profession in Prayer:
Heavenly Father, according to Psalm 39:1, the Psalmist knew that he could sin with his tongue. Give me self-control to control my mouth and keep me from evil speaking that does not agree with your Word. Thank you.

Promises—Professions

2 Corinthians 1:20
For no matter how many promises God has made, they are "Yes" in Christ. And so through him the "Amen" is spoken by us to the glory of God.

Profession in Prayer:
Heavenly Father, according to 2 Corinthians 1:20, Jesus has made all of your promises available to me when I decide in my spirit they are true. Every promise in your Word is mine. Praise Jesus!

Protection

1 Peter 1:5
. . . Through faith [we] are shielded by God's power until the coming of the salvation that is ready to be revealed in the last time.

Profession in Prayer:
Heavenly Father, according to 1 Peter 1:5, I am protected by the power of God; nothing can harm me!

John 10:27-30
"My sheep listen to my voice; I know them, and they

follow me. I give them eternal life, and they shall never perish; no one can snatch them out of my hand. My Father, who has given them to me, is greater than all; no one can snatch them out of my Father's hand. I and the Father are one."

Profession in Prayer:
Heavenly Father, according to John 10:27-30, you and Jesus are one. You are greater than all. No one shall ever snatch me from your protection and care. Thank you for the precious promise; I accept it.

Purity

2 Corinthians 7:1
Since we have these promises, dear friends, let us purify ourselves from everything that contaminates body and spirit, perfecting holiness out of reverence for God.

Profession in Prayer:
Heavenly Father, according to 2 Corinthians 7:1, I am to strive for perfection by purifying myself from evil. I choose to let the blood of Jesus cleanse me again, right now, in order that I might be a temple without sin that you are pleased to dwell in.

Qualified

Colossians 1:12
. . . giving thanks to the Father, who has qualified you to share in the inheritance of the saints in the kingdom of light.

Profession in Prayer:
Heavenly Father, according to Colossians 1:12, my

Father has qualified me to share in the inheritance of the saints in the light. I am a saint in the light, which is Christ, my Lord.

Rebuking Evil During Troubled Times

Psalm 6:2, 8, 9, 10

Be gracious to me, O Lord, for I am languishing; O Lord, heal me, for my bones are troubled. . . . Depart from me, all you workers of evil; for the Lord has heard . . . my supplication; the Lord accepts my prayer. All my enemies shall be ashamed and sorely troubled; they shall turn back, and be put to shame in a moment.

Profession in Prayer:

Heavenly Father, according to Psalm 6:2, 8, 9, 10, in this moment that I cry out to you in my distress, all the evil forces about me have fled. Bless your high and holy name.

Receiving the Kingdom

Luke 12:32-34

Do not be afraid, little flock, for your Father has been pleased to give you the kingdom. Sell your possessions and give to the poor. Provide purses for yourselves that will not wear out, a treasure in heaven that will not be exhausted, where no thief comes near and no moth destroys. For where your treasure is, there your heart will be also.

Profession in Prayer:

Heavenly Father, according to Luke 12:32-34, your

kingdom is much different from the world. Since I want my spirit to dwell in you, I will sell and give to the poor; in doing so my spirit will become united with your Holy Spirit and we will have no fear, for we have no earthly possessions to lose.

Reconcilers

2 Corinthians 5:19b, 20
. . . and he has committed to us the message of reconciliation. We are therefore Christ's ambassadors, as though God were making his appeal through us.

Profession in Prayer:
Heavenly Father, according to 2 Corinthians 5:19b, 20, you have given me the ministry of reconciliation. I profess that you are making your appeal to persons through me!

Redemption

Ephesians 1:7
In him we have redemption through his blood, the forgiveness of sins, in accordance with the riches of God's grace that he lavished on us, with all wisdom and understanding.

Profession in Prayer:
Heavenly Father, according to Ephesians 1:7, through the blood of Jesus I am redeemed out of the hands of the devil, I am forgiven, and I have wisdom and understanding.

Rejoicing

Psalm 16:8, 9
I keep the Lord always before me; because he is at

my right hand, I shall not be moved. Therefore my heart is glad, and my soul rejoices; my body also dwells secure.

Profession in Prayer:
Heavenly Father, according to Psalm 16:8, 9, because I glorify you my spirit is glad, my whole life rejoices, and my body dwells secure. I praise you.

Rest

Matthew 11:28-30
"Come to me, all you who are weary and burdened, and I will give you rest. Take my yoke upon you and learn from me, for I am gentle and humble in heart, and you will find rest for your souls. For my yoke is easy and my burden is light."

Profession in Prayer:
Heavenly Father, according to Matthew 11:28-30, I come to you, knowing you are gentle and humble. I trust you and receive rest.

Hebrews 4:3a
Now we who have believed enter that rest . . .

Profession in Prayer:
Heavenly Father, according to Hebrews 4:3, since I am exercising faith I am receiving rest in you.

Hebrews 4:1
Therefore, since the promise of entering his rest still stands. . . .

Profession in Prayer:
   Heavenly Father, according to Hebrews 4:1, your promise of rest still stands. I accept it. Thank you.

Restlessness

Hebrews 4:1, 2
   Therefore, since the promise of entering his rest still stands, let us be careful that none of you be found to have fallen short of it. For we also have had the gospel preached to us, just as they did; but the message they heard was of no value to them, because those who heard did not combine it with faith.

Profession in Prayer:
   Heavenly Father, according to Hebrews 4:1 and 2, the children of Israel did not exercise faith based upon your Word; therefore they were restless. I confess there have been times when I too forgot to mix faithing with your Word. Forgive me. Thanks. As I now exercise faith I receive rest.

Righteousness

Romans 4:21-24
   . . . being fully persuaded that God had power to do what he had promised. This is why "it was credited to him as righteousness." The words "it was credited to him" were written not for him alone, but also for us, to whom God will credit righteousness—for us who believe in him who raised Jesus our Lord from the dead.

Profession in Prayer:
   Heavenly Father, according to Romans 4:21-24, the

faith that I exercise into Jesus Christ is reckoned to me as righteousness.

Romans 5:17
For if, by the trespass of the one man, death reigned through that one man, how much more will those who receive God's abundant provision of grace and of the gift of righteousness reign in life through the one man, Jesus Christ.

Profession in Prayer:
Heavenly Father, according to Romans 5:17, through Jesus Christ, I am reigning in life. I am an overseer through Him.

Romans 6:13b
. . . but rather offer yourselves to God, as those who have been brought from death to life; and offer the parts of your body to him as instruments of righteousness.

Profession in Prayer:
Heavenly Father, according to Romans 6:13b, in Christ I am raised from the dead, and I present my members to you as instruments of righteousness.

---

2 Corinthians 9:10
Now he who supplies seed to the sower and bread for food will also supply and increase your store of seed and will enlarge the harvest of your righteousness.

Profession in Prayer:

Heavenly Father, according to 2 Corinthians 9:10, my Father is supplying and multiplying my seed for sowing (i.e., He is increasing my knowledge of the Word and my ability to use it correctly in every circumstance). He is increasing the harvest of my righteousness which is from Christ alone.

---

2 Corinthians 5:21

God made him who had no sin to be sin for us, so that in him we might become the righteousness of God.

Profession in Prayer:

Heavenly Father, according to 2 Corinthians 5:21, I am the righteousness of God in Christ. I am the righteousness of God in Christ because God's Word says so!

---

1 Peter 2:24

He himself bore our sins in his body on the tree, so that we might die to sins and live for righteousness; by his wounds you have been healed.

Profession in Prayer:

Heavenly Father, according to 1 Peter 2:24, through Jesus Christ, I have died to sin and now live to righteousness. I am healed.

Righteousness of God by Faithing

Romans 3:21-24

But now a righteousness from God, apart from law,

has been made known, to which the Law and the Prophets testify. This righteousness from God comes through faith in Jesus Christ to all who believe. There is no difference, for all have sinned and fall short of the glory of God, and are justified freely by his grace through the redemption that came by Christ Jesus.

Profession in Prayer:
Heavenly Father, according to Romans 3:21-24, through the blood of Jesus Christ, I am redeemed out of the hands of the devil and out of the kingdom of darkness. Through that redemption I have been freely justified, made just-as-if-I-had-not-sinned, by the grace of God.

Safety (Protection)

Romans 8:38, 39
For I am convinced that neither death nor life, neither angels nor demons, neither the present nor the future, nor any powers, neither height nor depth, nor anything else in all creation, will be able to separate us from the love of God that is in Christ Jesus our Lord.

Profession in Prayer:
Heavenly Father, according to Romans 3:38, 39, nothing can separate me from the love of God that is in Christ Jesus, my Lord—nothing!

Salvation

Romans 5:9
Since we have now been justified by his blood, how

much more shall we be saved from God's wrath through him!

Profession in Prayer:
Heavenly Father, according to Romans 5:9, through Jesus Christ, I shall be saved from the wrath of God to come.

Romans 10:9
That if you confess with your mouth, "Jesus is Lord," and believe in your heart that God raised him from the dead, you will be saved.

Profession in Prayer:
Heavenly Father, according to Romans 10:9, when I profess the Word, I am professing Jesus Christ. He is my Lord—I am saved! Hallelujah!

Romans 10:8b, 9
..."The word is near you; it is in your mouth and in your heart," that is, the word of faith we are proclaiming. That if you confess [profess] with your mouth, "Jesus is Lord," and believe in your heart that God raised him from the dead, you will be saved.

Profession in Prayer:
Heavenly Father, according to Romans 10:8b and 9, I have made a decision that God raised Jesus from the dead and that this same Jesus is my Lord. I am saved!

Sanctified—HOLY—Set Apart for Service

Hebrews 13:12
And so Jesus also suffered outside the city gate to

make his people holy through his own blood.

Profession in Prayer:
Heavenly Father, according to Hebrews 13:12, through the blood of Jesus I have been sanctified, made holy, set apart for service.

Hebrews 10:14
. . . because by one sacrifice he has made perfect forever those who are being made holy.

Profession in Prayer:
Heavenly Father, according to Hebrews 10:14, I have been perfected for all time through Jesus Christ, my offering unto God. In the mind of the Father, I am perfect in Christ.

Saved (continually)

Romans 5:10, 11
For if, when we were God's enemies, we were reconciled to him through the death of his Son, how much more, having been reconciled, shall we be saved through his life! Not only is this so, but we also rejoice in God through our Lord Jesus Christ, through whom we have now received reconciliation.

Profession in Prayer:
Heavenly Father, according to Romans 5:10, 11, through Jesus Christ, I have been reconciled to God, and I shall be saved by His life.

Security

Colossians 3:3
For you died, and your life is now hidden with Christ in God.

Profession in Prayer:
> Heavenly Father, according to Colossians 3:3, I have died and my life is hidden with Christ in God. Though the storm rages in the world, even though I am in the world, I am resting in the arms of you, Father. The victory has been won. The fight is over, forever.

Matthew 28:19, 20
> "Therefore go and make disciples of all nations, baptizing them in the name of the Father and of the Son and of the Holy Spirit, and teaching them to obey everything I have commanded you. And surely I will be with you always, to the very end of the age."

Profession in Prayer:
> Heavenly Father, according to Matthew 28:19, 20, as I go forth being a disciple and making disciples, you will never leave me alone, never. Thank you for this blessed assurance.

Self-Esteem

Romans 8:1, 2
> Therefore, there is now no condemnation for those who are in Christ Jesus, because through Christ Jesus the law of the Spirit of life set me free from the law of sin and death.

Profession in Prayer:
> Heavenly Father, according to Romans 8:1 and 2, I am in Christ and no longer under condemnation. The law of the Holy Spirit, which is life in Christ Jesus, has set me free from the law of sin and death. I am free!

Sin, Confession of

Psalm 32:8, 9
> I will instruct you and teach you the way you should go; I will counsel you with my eye upon you. Be not like a horse or a mule, without understanding, which must be curbed with bit and bridle, else it will not keep with you.

Profession in Prayer:
> Heavenly Father, I have comprehended Psalm 32:8 and 9. I confess that at times I have been stubborn and hard to guide like a horse or especially a mule. I receive your forgiveness and a soft pliable spirit to be taught. Now it will go well with you and me.

Romans 3:23, 24
> . . . for all have sinned and fall short of the glory of God, and are justified freely by his grace through the redemption that came by Christ Jesus.

Confession and Profession in Prayer:
> Heavenly Father, according to Romans 3:23, 24, all have sinned and fallen short of your glory. That includes me—I am sorry. However, I profess that I am justified freely; I am redeemed in Jesus. Hallelujah!

---

1 John 1:9
> If we confess our sins, he is faithful and just and will forgive us our sins and purify us from all unrighteousness.

Confession and Profession in Prayer:
Heavenly Father, according to 1 John 1:9, if I confess my sin you will forgive me and cleanse me from the works of Satan-unrighteousness. I do confess my sins, therefore I am forgiven and cleansed. Thank you.

Sons and Daughters of God

Romans 8:14
. . . those who are led by the Spirit of God are sons of God.

Profession in Prayer:
Heavenly Father, according to Romans 8:14, I am a son of God.

Romans 8:16
The Spirit himself testifies with our spirit that we are God's children.

Profession in Prayer:
Heavenly Father, according to Romans 8:16, your Holy Spirit testifies to my spirit and tells me that I am a son/daughter of God.

Shaken (Shook Up)

Acts 2:25-28
David said about him: " 'I saw the Lord always before me. Because he is at my right hand, I will not be shaken. Therefore my heart is glad and my tongue rejoices; my body also will live in hope,

because you will not abandon me to the grave, nor will you let your Holy One see decay. You have made known to me the paths of life; you will fill me with joy in your presence.'

Profession in Prayer:
   Heavenly Father, according to Acts 2:25-28, with David, I profess you are always before me. Therefore I am not shaken. My spirit is glad, I rejoice and have hope; you will never abandon me. Your presence fills me full with gladness because I know the ways of life.

Speech—Words

Psalm 15:1, 2
   O Lord, who shall sojourn in thy tent?
   Who shall dwell on thy holy hill?
   He who walks blamelessly, and does what is right,
   and speaks truth from his heart [spirit]. . . .

Profession in Prayer:
   Heavenly Father, according to Psalm 15: 1 and 2, I may live in your presence, since I am drawing upon your strength to walk blamelessly as I speak your Word, the ultimate truth.

Spiritual Blessings

Ephesians 1:3
   Praise be to the God and Father of our Lord Jesus Christ, who has blessed us in the heavenly realms with every spiritual blessing in Christ.

Profession in Prayer:
   Heavenly Father, according to Ephesians 1:3, I have

been blessed with every spiritual blessing in the heavenly places in Christ. It is true! I have been blessed and am being blessed as I dwell in Christ.

Strength

1 John 2:13, 14
I write to you, fathers, because you have known him who is from the beginning. I write to you, young men, because you have overcome the evil one. I write to you, dear children, because you have known the Father. I write to you, fathers, because you have known him who is from the beginning. I write to you, young men, because you are strong, and the word of God lives in you, and you have overcome the evil one.

Profession in Prayer:
Heavenly Father, according to 1 John 2:13, 14, the Lord is my strength. The Word of God abides in me, and through that Word I have overcome the evil one. I am his master in Christ!

Nehemiah 8:10b
. . . and do not be grieved, for the joy of the Lord is your strength.

Profession in Prayer:
Heavenly Father, according to Nehemiah 8:10b, the joy of the Lord is my strength.

Stability

Psalm 37:30, 31
The mouth of the righteous utters wisdom, and his

tongue speaks justice. The law of his God is in his heart; his steps do not slip.

Profession in Prayer:
Heavenly Father, according to Psalm 37:30, 31, my mouth utters wisdom and justice. Your Word is in my spirit, therefore my feet will not slip. I am secure.

Stress

James 1:12
Blessed is the man who perseveres under trial, because when he has stood the test, he will receive the crown of life that God has promised to those who love him.

Profession in Prayer:
Heavenly Father, according to James 1:12, I am blessed because of this trial. I will be blessed because I will be victorious over it. I will wear the victor's crown and you will receive the glory.

Psalm 9:9, 10
The Lord is a stronghold for the oppressed, a stronghold in times of trouble. And those who know thy name put their trust in thee, for thou, O Lord, has not forsaken those who trust thee.

Profession in Prayer:
Heavenly Father, according to Psalm 9:9, 10, you are my strength in this time of trouble and stress. You have never forsaken one person who exercised faith into you, and you will not forsake me. Glory!

Suffering

1 Peter 4:16
> However, if you suffer as a Christian, do not be ashamed, but praise God that you bear that name.

Profession in Prayer:
> Heavenly Father, according to 1 Peter 4:16, as I suffer for being a Christian, I praise you for allowing me the honor of suffering because of the name of Christ.

Romans 8:17
> Now if we are children, then we are heirs—heirs of God and co-heirs with Christ, if indeed we share in his sufferings in order that we may also share in his glory!

Profession in Prayer:
> Heavenly Father, according to Romans 8:17, I am a co-heir of you with Jesus. I share with Jesus' suffering. I am willing to suffer a share in his glory!

Sufficiency

2 Corinthians 12:9
> But he said to me, "My grace is sufficient for you, for my power is made perfect in weakness." Therefore, I will boast all the more gladly about my weaknesses, so that Christ's power may rest on me.

Profession in Prayer:
> Heavenly Father, according to 2 Corinthians 12:9, God's grace is sufficient for me; His power, or

ability, is perfected in my weakness. The ability of Christ dwells in me. I am weak in all things compared to Him—yet, in Christ, I am the ability of God!

Throne of God

Ephesians 2:18
> For through him we both have access to the Father by one Spirit.

Profession in Prayer:
> Heavenly Father, according to Ephesians 2:18, through Jesus Christ and in His Holy Spirit, I have access to you.

Transformed

2 Corinthians 3:18
> And we, who with unveiled faces all reflect the Lord's glory, are being transformed into his likeness with ever-increasing glory, which comes from the Lord, who is the Spirit.

Profession in Prayer:
> Heavenly Father, according to 2 Corinthians 3:18, as I look upon your face, and behold your glory, I am being transformed into your image, from glory to glory!

---

1 John 3:2b
> But we know that when he appears, we shall be like him, for we shall see him as he is.

Profession in Prayer:
   Heavenly Father, according to 1 John 3:2b, when Jesus appears, we shall be like Him, for even now we are being transformed into His likeness.

Triumph—Drawing Power

2 Corinthians 2:14-16
   But thanks be to God, who always leads us in triumphal procession in Christ and through us spreads everywhere the fragrance of the knowledge of him. For we are to God the aroma of Christ among those who are being saved and those who are perishing. To the one we are the smell of death; to the other, the fragrance of life. And who is equal to such a task?

Profession in Prayer:
   Heavenly Father, according to 2 Corinthians 2:14-16, I am the fragrance of Christ wherever I am. To the lost this is not pleasing when it reminds them that they are perishing. Yet I choose to exude this aroma since it will again give them the choice to come alive. Thank you for honoring me with your sweet fragrance that welcomes persons to know you. In Christ and by your Holy Spirit living in and through me I am adequate to the task.

Troubles

2 Corinthians 4:16-18
   Therefore we do not lose heart. Though outwardly we are wasting away, yet inwardly we are being renewed day by day. For our light and momentary

troubles are achieving for us an eternal glory that far outweighs them all. So we fix our eyes not on what is seen, but on what is unseen. For what is seen is temporary, but what is unseen is eternal.

Profession in Prayer:
Heavenly Father, according to 2 Corinthians 4:16-18, my troubles are momentary and light. They seem heavy at times, but the eternal glory you are preparing for me far outweighs them. I am fixing my eyes on Jesus, who is eternal.

Unfaithing

Hebrews 3:12, 13
See to it, brothers, that none of you has a sinful, unbelieving heart that turns away from the living God. But encourage one another daily, as long as it is called Today, so that none of you may be hardened by sin's deceitfulness.

Profession in Prayer:
Heavenly Father, according to Hebrews 3:12 and 13, I profess that this fact is true for me. I will turn from unfaithing, from depending on circumstances and feelings. I will encourage my brethren so that none may be hardened or deceived by sin.

Victory

Romans 6:14
For sin shall not be your master, because you are not under law, but under grace.

Profession in Prayer:
Heavenly Father, according to Romans 6:14, through Jesus Christ sin shall not be a master over me; I am master over sin.

---

1 John 4:4
You, dear children, are from God and have overcome them, because the one who is in you is greater than the one who is in the world.

Profession in Prayer:
Heavenly Father, according to 1 John 4:4, in Christ I am of God and have overcome the forces of darkness. Greater is His Holy Spirit who is in me than he who is in the world. Hallelujah, it is a fact!

---

1 John 2:13, 14
I write to you, fathers, because you have known him who is from the beginning. I write to you, young men, because you have overcome the evil one. I write to you, dear children, because you have known the Father. I write to you, fathers, because you have known him who is from the beginning. I write to you, young men, because you are strong, and the word of God lives in you, and you have overcome the evil one.

Profession in Prayer:
Heavenly Father, according to 1 John 2:13 and 14, the Lord is my strength. The Word of God abides in me, and through that Word I have overcome the evil one. I am his master in Christ!

Warfare

1 John 4:4
You, dear children, are from God and have overcome them, because the one who is in you is greater than the one who is in the world.

Profession in Prayer:
Heavenly Father, according to 1 John 4:4, in Christ I am of God and have overcome the forces of darkness. Greater is He who is in me than he who is in the world! Hallelujah!

---

1 John 5:4
... for everyone born of God has overcome the world. This is the victory that has overcome the world, even our faith.

Profession in Prayer:
Heavenly Father, according to 1 John 5:4, by faithing into Christ I have overcome the world and its influences. I am existing for God, my Father, through Jesus Christ, my Lord.

Weaknesses

Romans 8:26
In the same way, the Spirit helps us in our weakness.

Profession in Prayer:
Heavenly Father, according to Romans 8:26, your Holy Spirit helps me when I confess my weakness. I am receiving your help right now.

Weapons for Victory

2 Corinthians 10:4, 5

The weapons we fight with are not the weapons of the world. On the contrary, they have divine power to demolish strongholds. We demolish arguments and every pretension that sets itself up against the knowledge of God, and we take captive every thought to make it obedient to Christ.

Profession in Prayer:

Heavenly Father, according to 2 Corinthians 10:4 and 5, the weapons I fight with are divinely powerful for tearing down strongholds. In Christ I am equipped to take every thought captive and make it obedient to Christ. My weapons are the words of God in holy Scripture.

Weariness

1 Corinthians 15:58

Therefore, my dear brothers, stand firm. Let nothing move you. Always give yourselves fully to the work of the Lord, because you know that your labor in the Lord is not in vain.

Profession in Prayer:

Heavenly Father, according to 1 Corinthians 15:58, you are the triumphant One, and my work in you is not in vain. I can give myself fully knowing that you are at work in and through me.

Romans 8:11

And if the Spirit of him who raised Jesus from the dead is living in you, he who raised Christ from the dead will also give life to your mortal bodies through his Spirit, who lives in you.

Profession in Prayer:
Heavenly Father, according to Romans 8:11, I am not weary or tired, I am not dead within. The Holy Spirit within me has given my mortal body life in order that I may do the will of God.

Wisdom

James 1:5
If any of you lacks wisdom, he should ask God, who gives generously to all without finding fault, and it will be given to him.

Profession in Prayer:
Heavenly Father, according to James 1:5, if I ask you, you will give me wisdom. Therefore I ask for and receive wisdom.

Wisdom, Understanding and Knowledge

Proverbs 2:1-12
My son, if you receive my words and treasure up my commandments with you, making your ear attentive to wisdom and inclining your heart to understanding; yes, if you cry out for insight and raise your voice for understanding, if you seek it like silver and search for it as for hidden treasures; then you will understand the fear of the Lord and find the knowledge of God. For the Lord gives wisdom; from his mouth come knowledge and understanding; he stores up sound wisdom for the upright; he is a shield to those

who walk in integrity, guarding the paths of justice and preserving the way of his saints. Then you will understand righteousness and justice and equity, every good path; for wisdom will come into your heart, and knowledge will be pleasant to your soul; discretion will watch over you; understanding will guard you; delivering you from the way of evil, from men of perverted speech.

Profession in Prayer:
Heavenly Father, according to Proverbs 2:1-12, as I receive and profess your Word, I have wisdom in my spirit, knowledge is pleasant to my life, and your discretion and understanding is guarding me. Praise you, Father, for your most holy and powerful Word.

Word

1 Thessalonians 2:13b
. . . when you received the word of God, which you heard from us, you accepted it not as the word of men, but as it actually is, the word of God, which is at work in you who believe.

Profession in Prayer:
Heavenly Father, according to 1 Thessalonians 2:13b, God's Word operates in me and through me as I act on it. As I act on the Word, I am putting His will into operation.

John 5:24
"I tell you the truth, whoever hears my word and believes him who sent me has eternal life and will

not be condemned; he has crossed over from death to life.

Profession in Prayer:
Heavenly Father, according to John 5:24, I have eternal life in Jesus. I have passed from death into life everlasting.

James 1:21
Therefore, get rid of all moral filth and the evil that is so prevalent, and humbly accept the word planted in you, which can save you.

Profession in Prayer:
Heavenly Father, according to James 1:21, your Word planted in me will continually save me as I willfully reject moral filth and evil. Praise be to Jesus!

James 1:22-25
Do not merely listen to the word, and so deceive yourselves. Do what it says. Anyone who listens to the word but does not do what it says is like a man who looks at his face in a mirror and, after looking at himself, goes away and immediately forgets what he looks like. But the man who looks intently into the perfect law that gives freedom, and continues to do this, not forgetting what he has heard, but doing it—he will be blessed in what he does.

Profession in Prayer:
Heavenly Father, according to James 1:22-25, I have freedom because I am continuing to look intently

into your Word and am continually striving to be obedient to it. I will be blessed in what I do.

Wrath Turned Away

Proverbs 15:1, 2 and 4
A soft answer turns away wrath, but a harsh word stirs up anger. The tongue of the wise dispenses knowledge, but the mouths of fools pour out folly. . . . A gentle tongue is a tree of life, but perverseness in it breaks the spirit.

Profession in Prayer:
Heavenly Father, according to Proverbs 15:1, 2 and 4, as I answer softly and meekly in love, wrath will not come upon me. My gentle tongue is a tree of life, Hallelujah!

Worship

Philippians 3:3
For it is we who are the circumcision, we who worship by the Spirit of God, who glory in Christ Jesus, and who put no confidence in the flesh. . . .

Profession in Prayer:
Heavenly Father, according to Philippians 3:3, I am the true circumcision. I worship in the Spirit, I glory in Christ Jesus, and I put no confidence in the flesh.

Index

Verses and Professions

Access Into the Holy of Holies
for Worship
   Hebrews 10:19-22
Adequacy
   2 Corinthians 3:4-6
Aging
   Psalm 92:13-15
Alive
   Romans 6:8-11
   Romans 6:22, 23
   Romans 8:10
   Romans 8:11
   Galatians 2:20
   Ephesians 2:4-6
   1 Peter 1:23
   2 Peter 1:3
   1 John 2:23
   John 10:10
Ambassadors
   2 Corinthians 5:20
Angels
   1 Peter 3:21b, 22
Anger
   Proverbs 16:32
   Romans 12:18-21
   Ephesians 4:26, 27
   Colossians 3:7, 8
   James 1:19, 20
   Psalm 4:4
Anxiety
   Psalm 37:3, 4
   Psalm 37:5, 6
   Matthew 6:25-27
   Matthew 6:31-34
   Matthew 11:28-30
   Romans 9:33
   Philippians 4:6-8
   Hebrews 13:5b, 6
   1 Peter 5:6, 7
Blessings
   Galatians 3:7
   Galatians 3:9
   Galatians 3:13, 14
Blood of Jesus
   Ephesians 1:7
   1 John 1:7
   Romans 5:9
   Hebrews 9:14
   1 Peter 1:18, 19
   Hebrews 10:19, 20

Hebrews 13:12
Hebrews 13:15
1 Corinthians 6:19, 20
Colossians 1:19, 20
Buried With Christ
   Romans 6:3, 4
Characteristics of God
   Romans 7:4
   Romans 8:23
   Galatians 5:22, 23
Children of God
   Romans 8:14
   Romans 8:16, 17
   1 John 3:1
Chosen
   Ephesians 1:4
   1 Peter 2:9
Cleansing From Sin
   1 John 1:7
Complete
   Colossians 2:10
Confidence
   Philippians 1:20
   Philippians 1:6
Confusion
   1 Corinthians 6:3
   1 Corinthians 6:12
Conscience—Inner Healing
   Hebrews 9:14
Continually Saved
   Romans 5:10, 11
Correction—Chastening
   Hebrews 12:10
Criticism
   Romans 14:13
Daily Strength
   Psalm 68:19
Death
   John 8:51
Deliverance From Empty Ways of Life
   1 Peter 1:18, 19
Delivered
   Romans 6:6, 7
Depression
   Psalm 43:5
   Isaiah 41:10
   Philippians 4:8
Divine Nature
   2 Peter 1:4
Drawing Power
   2 Corinthians 9:14
Dwelling Place of God
   1 Corinthians 3:16
   1 Corinthians 6:13b
   1 Corinthians 6:19, 20
Energized
   Philippians 2:13
   Philippians 4:13
Eternal Life
   1 John 5:13
   1 Corinthians 15:54, 55
Faithing
   Romans 4:23, 24
Failure
   Philippians 3:12-14
Family of God
   Ephesians 2:19
Fear
   1 John 4:18
   Psalm 27:1
   Psalm 46:1, 2a
Fellowship With God
   1 John 1:3
   1 John 1:7
Finances
   Hebrews 13:5-7
Forgiven
   Colossians 2:13, 14
Forgiving Others
   Proverbs 17:9

Freedom
  Romans 8:12
  Galatians 5:1
  John 8:36
Freedom From Oppression—
Security
  Psalm 17:1-5
Freedom From Sin
  1 John 5:18
Fruit Bearing
  John 15:5
Gladness
  1 Chronicles 29:11-13
  Philippians 1:20
Good Works
  Ephesians 2:10
Guidance
  Psalm 25:10
  Psalm 25:12
  Proverbs 16:9
  Proverbs 16:1-3
  Proverbs 3:5, 6
  Psalm 32:8, 9
Healing
  Isaiah 53:4, 5
  Matthew 8:16, 17
  1 Peter 2:24
Help in Testing
  1 Corinthians 10:13
  Hebrews 4:14-16
Holy Spirit
  Romans 7:6
  1 Corinthians 2:12
  Titus 3:5, 6
  Galatians 3:13, 14b
  Galatians 5:16
  Ephesians 1:13, 14
Insults
  Matthew 5:11, 12
  1 Peter 4:14

Jesus
  1 Peter 1:21
Joy
  Galatians 5:22
Justification—Just-As-If-I'd-
Never-Sinned
  Romans 5:9
  Romans 3:28
Laziness
  Hebrews 6:12
Liberty
  2 Corinthians 3:17
Life by Profession of the Mouth
  Proverbs 18:20, 21
Love
  Romans 5:5
  2 Corinthians 5:14
  2 Timothy 1:7
  1 John 2:10
  1 Corinthians 13:4-8a
  Galatians 5:22a
  1 John 4:7, 8
  Romans 5:5
Mind (Sphere) of Christ
  1 Corinthians 2:16
Mind, Sphere, *Nous*—Renewed
  Romans 12:1, 2
Needs
  2 Corinthians 9:8
  Philippians 4:19
  Hebrews 4:16
New Beginning
  2 Corinthians 5:17
New Creation
  Ephesians 4:22-24
Patience
  James 5:7, 8
  Galatians 5:22, 23a
  Galatians 6:9

Peace
    Colossians 1:19, 20
    Romans 5:1
    Ephesians 2:13, 14a
    Galatians 5:22
    Colossians 3:15
Peacemakers
    James 3:18
    Romans 8:15
Perfect Before the Father
    Hebrews 10:10 and 14
Possibilities
    Matthew 17:20b, 21
    Mark 9:23b
    Luke 18:27
Praise Professions
    Psalm 7:17
    Psalm 9:1, 2
Pride
    Romans 12:6-8
Profession
    Psalm 37:30, 31
Profession, Evil
    Psalm 39:1
Promises—Professions
    2 Corinthians 1:20
Protection
    1 Peter 1:5
    John 10:27-30
Purity
    2 Corinthians 7:1
Qualified
    Colossians 1:12
Rebuking Evil During
Troubled Times
    Psalm 6:2, 8, 9, 10
Receiving the Kingdom
    Luke 12:32-34
Reconcilers
    2 Corinthians 5:19b, 20

Redemption
    Ephesians 1:7
Rejoicing
    Psalm 16:8, 9
Rest
    Matthew 11:28-30
    Hebrews 4:3a
    Hebrews 4:1
Restlessness
    Hebrews 4:1, 2
Righteousness
    Romans 4:21-24
    Romans 5:17
    Romans 6:13b
    2 Corinthians 9:10
    2 Corinthians 5:21
    1 Peter 2:24
Righteousness of God by
Faithing
    Romans 3:21-24
Safety (Protection)
    Romans 8:38, 39
Salvation
    Romans 5:9
    Romans 10:9
    Romans 10:8b, 9
Sanctified—HOLY—Set Apart
for Service
    Hebrews 13:12
    Hebrews 10:14
Saved (continually)
    Romans 5:10, 11
Security
    Colossians 3:3
    Matthew 28:19, 20
Self-Esteem
    Romans 8:1, 2
Sin, Confession of
    Psalm 32:8, 9
    Romans 3:23, 24
    1 John 1:9

Sons and Daughters of God
   Romans 8:14
   Romans 8:16
Shaken (Shook Up)
   Acts 2:25-28
Speech—Words
   Psalm 15:1, 2
Spiritual Blessings
   Ephesians 1:3
Strength
   1 John 2:13, 14
   Nehemiah 8:10b
Stability
   Psalm 37:30, 31
Stress
   James 1:12
   Psalm 9:9, 10
Suffering
   1 Peter 4:16
   Romans 8:17
Sufficiency
   2 Corinthians 12:9
Throne of God
   Ephesians 2:18
Transformed
   2 Corinthians 3:18
   1 John 3:2b
Triumph—Drawing Power
   2 Corinthians 2:14-16
Troubles
   2 Corinthians 4:16-18
Unfaithing
   Hebrews 3:12, 13
Victory
   Romans 6:14
   1 John 4:4
   1 John 2:13, 14
Warfare
   1 John 4:4
   1 John 5:4

Weaknesses
   Romans 8:26
Weapons for Victory
   2 Corinthians 10:4, 5
Weariness
   1 Corinthians 15:58
   Romans 8:11
Wisdom
   James 1:5
Wisdom, Understanding and Knowledge
   Proverbs 2:1-12
Word
   1 Thessalonians 2:13b
   John 5:24
   James 1:21
   James 1:22-25
Wrath Turned Away
   Proverbs 15:1, 2 and 4
Worship
   Philippians 3:3